PARTY FARE

◆

Reader's Digest Healthy Cooking Library

PARTY FARE

Reader's
Digest

Published by The Reader's Digest Association Limited

LONDON ◆ NEW YORK ◆ SYDNEY ◆ CAPE TOWN ◆ MONTREAL

The Reader's Digest Healthy Cooking Library was edited and
designed by The Reader's Digest Association Ltd, London.
These recipes and illustrations have previously appeared in
GREAT RECIPES FOR GOOD HEALTH, published in 1993
by Reader's Digest, UK.

First Edition

Printed in Italy

ISBN 0 276 42175 2

Consultant Editor Pat Alburey
Nutritional Consultant Editor Cynthia Robinson, BSc
Nutritional Consultant Moya de Wet, BSc, SRD

Recipes created by Pat Alburey, Valerie Barrett, Jackie Burrow,
Carole Handslip, Petra Jackson, Meg Jansz, Angela Kingsbury,
Danielle Nay, Louise Pickford, Jane Suthering, Judith Taylor,
Hilaire Walden

CONTENTS

COCKTAIL SNACKS AND DRINKS

Light bites and imaginative drinks set parties and celebratory dinners off with a swing. This selection has something for every season and social occasion – and all, from spicy toasted nuts and savoury dips to turkey bouchées and stuffed tomatoes, have been vetted for sugar and fat. There is redcurrant punch to take the chill off winter evenings, an icy spritzer to refresh in the summer sun, and hot chocolate with a difference to make a soothing pick-me-up.

Turkey bouchées

ONE BOUCHÉE

CALORIES 50

TOTAL FAT 2g

  SATURATED FAT 1g

CARBOHYDRATES 2g

  ADDED SUGAR 0

FIBRE 0

SODIUM 45mg

MAKES 24
PREPARATION TIME: 25 minutes
COOKING TIME: 20 minutes
OVEN: Preheat to 180°C (350°F, gas mark 4)

1 tablespoon olive oil
2 small carrots, peeled and finely diced
1 medium onion, peeled and finely chopped
½ small green pepper, de-seeded and finely chopped
½ small red pepper, de-seeded and finely chopped

1 level teaspoon dried rubbed sage
1 egg, size 2, lightly beaten
1lb (450g) minced uncooked turkey
2oz (60g) wholemeal breadcrumbs
2 tablespoons tomato purée
2oz (60g) grated Gruyère cheese
Freshly ground black pepper
24 unsalted pistachio nuts, shelled and skinned
½ level teaspoon paprika

Attractive little bouchées, or mouthfuls, of turkey, speckled and moistened with carrot, onion and pepper, are given extra flavour by Gruyère and pistachios.

1 Heat the oil in a heavy-based saucepan and cook the carrots, onion, green and red pepper and sage in it, covered, over a low heat for 10 minutes, stirring occasionally.

2 Turn into a large bowl and mix in the egg, turkey, breadcrumbs, tomato purée and Gruyère. Season with pepper.

3 Spoon the mixture into small-cup nonstick bun trays, half-filling each cup. Place a

pistachio nut on each bouchée. Cook in the heated oven for about 20 minutes, or until the bouchées are golden and firm, and there is no trace of pink in the juice that oozes out when they are tested with a fine skewer or a fork.

4 Leave to cool slightly, then lift out the bouchées carefully. Serve them immediately while hot, or cool and refrigerate for up to 4 hours. Sprinkle lightly with the paprika just before serving.

Iced apple-mint tea

MAKES 4 GLASSES
PREPARATION TIME: 5 minutes,
plus 20 minutes to infuse

1 pint (570ml) boiling water
2 Ceylon tea bags
3 level tablespoons chopped fresh apple-mint leaves
1 wide strip lemon rind
¾ pint (425ml) dry cider, well chilled
1 tablespoon lemon juice
12-20 ice cubes
4 sprigs mint and 4 lemon slices for decoration

1   Pour the boiling water into a warmed teapot with the tea bags, mint and lemon rind. Cover and leave to infuse for 20 minutes, then remove and discard the tea bags.

2   Strain the tea into a large jug and stir in the cider, lemon juice and half the ice.

3   Share the remaining ice between four tumblers and pour equal amounts of mint tea into each glass. Stir briskly and garnish each glass with a mint sprig and a slice of lemon.

ONE GLASS
CALORIES 40
TOTAL FAT 0
SATURATED FAT 0
CARBOHYDRATES 0
ADDED SUGAR 0
FIBRE 0
SODIUM 10mg

TIP
You can make decorative ice cubes for this drink by adding mint leaves to the cubes before freezing.

Mint and lemon, among the freshest of all tastes, combine with fragrant tea and cider to create a long, cooling drink for sunny summer days.

Savoury biscuits

MAKES 24
PREPARATION TIME: 1 hour,
plus 15 minutes to rise
COOKING TIME: 15 minutes
OVEN: Preheat to 180°C (350°F, gas mark 4)

4fl oz (115ml) lukewarm skimmed milk
¼ level teaspoon caster sugar
1 level teaspoon dried yeast
8oz (225g) plain flour
⅛ level teaspoon salt
1oz (30g) polyunsaturated margarine, melted
2 level teaspoons each sesame seeds and poppy seeds

1 Pour the milk into a bowl, stir in the sugar until it dissolves, then whisk in the yeast. Cover and leave in a warm place for about 10 minutes until frothy.

2 Sift the flour and salt into a bowl and make a well in the centre. Pour in the yeast liquid and the melted margarine. Mix to form a slightly dry dough; do not add any extra liquid.

3 Turn the dough onto a lightly floured surface and knead for about 6 minutes, until smooth and springy. Put the dough in a clean bowl, cover with a clean, damp teacloth and leave to rise in a warm place for 15 minutes.

4 Roll the dough out to form an oblong about 18×6in (46×15cm) long. Working from a narrow end, fold the bottom third of the dough up and over the centre third, then bring the top third down over it. Press the edges firmly together with the rolling pin.

5 Give the dough a quarter turn and roll it out to the large oblong again, then fold as before. Repeat seven more times.

6 Roll the pastry out to ⅛ in (3mm) thick and prick with a fork, pricking at close intervals all over the dough. Cut out rounds with a 3in (75mm) plain biscuit cutter. Place the rounds on ungreased baking sheets.

7 Put together the trimmings, overlapping them to form an oblong, then roll out to ⅛ in (3mm) thick and cut out more rounds.

8 Lightly brush the rounds with cold water. Sprinkle one half with sesame seeds and the other with poppy seeds, pressing the seeds down lightly with the back of a spoon. Bake in the heated oven for 15 minutes, or until lightly browned. Remove the biscuits from the oven and immediately cool on wire racks. They will keep well in an airtight container.

ONE BISCUIT	
CALORIES 45	
TOTAL FAT 2g	
SATURATED FAT 0	
CARBOHYDRATES 6g	
ADDED SUGAR 0	
FIBRE 0	
SODIUM 25mg	

Sesame snaps

MAKES 30
PREPARATION TIME: 20 minutes
COOKING TIME: 15 minutes
OVEN: Preheat to 180°C (350°F, gas mark 4)

8oz (225g) plain wholemeal flour
⅛ level teaspoon salt
½ level teaspoon baking powder
2oz (60g) polyunsaturated margarine
1oz (30g) sesame seeds
4 tablespoons skimmed milk
1 egg white, size 2
1 level teaspoon paprika

1 Sift the flour, salt and baking powder into a bowl, tipping in the bran left in the sieve. Rub in the margarine, stir in half the sesame seeds and make a well in the centre.

2 Set aside ½ tablespoon of the milk. Lightly beat the rest with the egg white and pour into the well. Mix to a firm, even-textured dough.

3 Roll out on a lightly floured surface until ⅛ in (3mm) thick. Cut with a sharp knife into 3×1½ in (75×40mm) oblongs.

4 Arrange well spaced out on lightly greased baking sheets. Knead and roll out the pastry trimmings to cut into more oblongs.

5 Brush the biscuits with the reserved milk and sprinkle the remaining sesame seeds and the paprika on top. Bake in the heated oven for about 15 minutes, or until lightly browned. Put the biscuits on wire racks to cool before storing in an airtight tin.

ONE BISCUIT	
CALORIES 40	
TOTAL FAT 2g	
SATURATED FAT 0	
CARBOHYDRATES 4g	
ADDED SUGAR 0	
FIBRE 1g	
SODIUM 30mg	

Home-baked flaky and wholemeal biscuits offer a crisp and light alternative to bread. Enjoy them with cheese, pâtés, dips and spreads.

Chickpea and rosemary dip

MAKES 18 level tablespoons
PREPARATION TIME: 20 minutes,
plus 1 hour to refrigerate

7oz (200g) cooked chickpeas
1 level teaspoon chopped fresh rosemary,
or ½ level teaspoon dried rosemary
2 level teaspoons chopped fresh parsley
1 small clove garlic, peeled and crushed
1 small red onion, peeled and finely chopped
2 teaspoons lime juice
1-4 tablespoons vegetable stock
Freshly ground black pepper
¼ level teaspoon paprika
Sprigs of fresh rosemary to garnish

LEVEL TABLESPOON	
CALORIES	15
TOTAL FAT	0
SATURATED FAT	0
CARBOHYDRATES	2g
ADDED SUGAR	0
FIBRE	1g
SODIUM	0

1 Blend the chickpeas, rosemary, parsley and garlic in a food processor for 30 seconds to make a smooth purée.

2 Mix in the onion and lime juice and stir in enough stock to give the dip the consistency of thick whipped cream. Season with pepper.

3 Turn the dip into a serving bowl, sprinkle with paprika and garnish with the rosemary sprigs. Cover and refrigerate for 1 hour, or up to 3 hours, before serving.

Serve with fingers of toast, pitta bread triangles, savoury biscuits, or raw vegetables.

Cottage cheese and basil dip

MAKES 18 level tablespoons
PREPARATION TIME: 15 minutes,
plus 1 hour to refrigerate

10oz (275g) cottage cheese, drained
6 medium radishes, trimmed and finely chopped
2 level tablespoons chopped fresh basil,
or 1 level teaspoon dried basil
1 clove garlic, peeled and crushed
½ level teaspoon finely grated lemon rind
Basil leaves and 2-3 radish flowers to garnish

LEVEL TABLESPOON	
CALORIES	15
TOTAL FAT	0
SATURATED FAT	0
CARBOHYDRATES	1g
ADDED SUGAR	0
FIBRE	0
SODIUM	60mg

1 Blend the cheese in a food processor for 20 seconds, or pass it through a nylon sieve.

2 Stir the chopped radishes, basil, garlic and lemon rind into the cheese. Spoon the mixture into a serving bowl, cover and refrigerate for 1 hour, or up to 3 hours, before serving.

3 Garnish the dip with the basil leaves and radish flowers.

Guacamole

MAKES 18 level tablespoons
PREPARATION TIME: 20 minutes

1 large ripe avocado, halved, stoned and peeled
2 level tablespoons low-fat natural yoghurt
2 medium tomatoes, skinned, de-seeded and chopped
2 level tablespoons chopped fresh parsley
or coriander
½ level teaspoon ground coriander
1 small red onion, peeled and finely chopped
4 teaspoons lime or lemon juice
1 clove garlic, peeled and crushed
Coriander leaves to garnish

LEVEL TABLESPOON	
CALORIES	25
TOTAL FAT	2g
SATURATED FAT	0
CARBOHYDRATES	1g
ADDED SUGAR	0
FIBRE	1g
SODIUM	5mg

1 Mash the avocado with a fork in a bowl, until it becomes smooth and creamy. Stir in all the other ingredients gently but thoroughly.

2 Spoon the guacamole into a serving bowl, garnish with coriander leaves and serve at once, or cover and refrigerate for up to 30 minutes. Do not keep the dip any longer or it will start to blacken.

You can serve savoury biscuits or Melba toast with the guacamole, or pack it into short lengths of celery.

An assortment of crudités provides edible scoops for three delicious dips: coriander, onion and tomato add flavour and body to guacamole (near right); the mild, nutty flavour of chickpeas is sharpened with lime and rosemary (centre); and cottage cheese is given a peppery bite by chopped radishes and a seasoning of fresh basil.

TIP
To make a radish flower, slice off the stalk end, stand the radish cut end down and trim off the tip. Make rows of deep cuts round the radish, cutting downwards. Put it in iced water in the refrigerator for 30 minutes and the cuts will open up.

Courgette and cheese wheels

MAKES 30 wheels
PREPARATION TIME: 15 minutes,
plus 1 hour to refrigerate

2oz (60g) low-fat cottage cheese, drained
and passed through a nylon sieve
2oz (60g) ricotta cheese
1 level teaspoon each chopped fresh basil, chives
and thyme
2 large courgettes, each about 4oz (115g),
washed and trimmed
Whole mixed peppercorns (pink, green,
white and black)
Thyme or parsley to garnish

1 Mix the cottage cheese and ricotta cheese
with the basil, chives and thyme. Using a potato
peeler, cut the courgettes lengthways into thin
slices. Discard the narrow first and last slices of
each courgette.

2 Spread each courgette slice with cheese
mixture and roll up neatly. Lay them close
together in a shallow dish, cover and refrigerate
for at least 1 hour and up to 3 hours.

3 Arrange the wheels on a serving plate. Grind
the pepper over them, garnish with thyme or
parsley and serve.

Mushrooms with watercress stuffing

MAKES 12
PREPARATION TIME: 20 minutes
COOKING TIME: 10 minutes
OVEN: Preheat to 200°C (400°F, gas mark 6)

12 medium open-cap mushrooms, wiped
and trimmed
2 tablespoons olive oil
2 cloves garlic, peeled and crushed
2 bunches watercress, trimmed, washed and chopped
½ level teaspoon dried oregano
1 tablespoon lemon juice
1½ oz (45g) wholemeal breadcrumbs
3 slices wholemeal bread
1 level tablespoon chopped fresh thyme or chives

1 Separate the stalks from the mushrooms
and chop them, leaving the cups whole. Heat
half the oil in a frying pan and cook half the
garlic in it over a moderate heat for 30 seconds.
Stir in the mushroom stalks and cook for about
5 minutes, until lightly coloured.

2 Mix in the watercress and oregano, and cook
for about 1 minute, until the watercress wilts.
Sprinkle in the lemon juice and remove the pan
from the heat.

3 Fill the mushrooms with the stuffing and
top with the breadcrumbs. Arrange the
mushrooms on a nonstick baking tray and cook
in the heated oven for about 10 minutes, or
until the breadcrumbs are lightly browned and
the mushrooms softened.

4 Meanwhile, mix the remaining oil and
garlic with the thyme or chives. Toast the bread
on one side under the grill, then brush the oil
mixture over the other side and toast until
lightly coloured.

5 Using a plain round biscuit cutter about
the same size as the mushrooms, stamp out
12 small rounds from the toast. Set a
mushroom on each and serve immediately.

Spicy toasted nuts

MAKES 15 level tablespoons
PREPARATION TIME: 20 minutes

3½ oz (100g) shelled almonds
6 cardamom pods

¾ level teaspoon ground cumin
¾ level teaspoon ground coriander
⅛ level teaspoon cayenne pepper
1 teaspoon olive oil
3½ oz (100g) unsalted cashew nuts

1 Put the almonds into a saucepan, cover with cold water, bring to the boil and drain immediately. Slide off and discard the skins.

2 Take the cardamom seeds from their pods and crush them. Mix in the cumin, coriander and cayenne pepper.

3 Heat the oil in a frying pan and stir-fry the nuts in it over a moderate heat for about 3 minutes, until golden, as if lightly toasted.

4 Mix in the spices and stir over the heat for 30 seconds. Turn into a heatproof dish and leave until cold before serving.

Colourful spirals of paper-thin courgette slices holding soft cheese make an attractive show on party platters; baked mushrooms filled with hot watercress and oregano have a crisp crumb topping and sit on discs of toast; almonds and cashew nuts take on a richer colour and flavour when tossed with a coating of spices.

Freshwater prawns in spiced dressing

ONE PRAWN	
CALORIES	20
TOTAL FAT	1g
SATURATED FAT	0
CARBOHYDRATES	1g
ADDED SUGAR	0
FIBRE	0
SODIUM	25mg

TIP
To de-vein a prawn, make a shallow cut along its back and lift out the fine black vein with the tip of the knife.

MAKES 24
PREPARATION TIME: 30 minutes, plus 2-3 hours to cool and refrigerate
COOKING TIME: 20 minutes

12 whole black peppercorns
12 coriander seeds
4 cloves
1 bay leaf
½ level teaspoon mustard seeds
½ level teaspoon dried thyme
1 medium onion, peeled and chopped
1 stick celery, trimmed and chopped
3 slices lemon
3 cloves garlic, peeled and chopped
2 tablespoons white wine vinegar
24 large raw freshwater prawns, about 1¼ lb (550g) together, peeled, de-veined, tails left on
2 tablespoons lemon juice
1 tablespoon virgin olive oil
⅛ level teaspoon cayenne pepper
Lemon and lime slices and dill fronds to garnish

1 Put the peppercorns, coriander seeds, cloves, bay leaf, mustard seeds and thyme in a small square of muslin or white cotton fabric, gather the sides together and tie securely with clean thread.

2 Bring 1¼ pints (725ml) of unsalted water to the boil in a large stainless steel or enamel saucepan and add the onion, celery, lemon slices, garlic, vinegar and the bag of spices. Reduce the heat and simmer, uncovered, for 15 minutes.

3 Pour in the prawns and cook, uncovered, for 2-3 minutes, stirring frequently, until they turn pink. Remove from the heat and leave to cool in the pan, then cover and refrigerate for 2 hours.

4 Drain the prawns and discard the lemon slices and spices. Gently toss the prawns, onion and celery with the lemon juice, oil and cayenne. Turn into a serving dish and garnish with slices of lemon, lime and dill.

Remember to put a supply of cocktail sticks on the table beside the prawns.

Stuffed radishes

THREE RADISHES	
CALORIES	15
TOTAL FAT	0
SATURATED FAT	0
CARBOHYDRATES	1g
ADDED SUGAR	0
FIBRE	0
SODIUM	10mg

MAKES about 30
PREPARATION TIME: 15 minutes, plus 30 minutes to refrigerate

2 bunches radishes, washed and trimmed, leaving a little stalk on each
4oz (115g) quark or low-fat cottage cheese
⅛ level teaspoon cayenne pepper, or 1 level teaspoon celery seeds
1 level teaspoon poppy seeds

1 Cut downwards through the centre tip of each radish three times, making a star pattern and cutting almost to the stalk. Put the radishes in iced water in the refrigerator for 30 minutes, or until they open into a flower shape.

2 Mix the cheese with the cayenne pepper or celery seeds; if using cottage cheese, pass it through a sieve first. Pipe the mixture through a small star nozzle into the centre of each radish, or press it in with a knife.

3 Sprinkle the radishes with poppy seeds and arrange on a serving dish. Serve them at once, or keep in the refrigerator, covered, for up to 2 hours. Take them out about 30 minutes before serving time.

Meaty prawns are flavoured with a subtle infusion of herbs, spices and vegetables while they cook, and then given a hot cayenne dressing; pretty radishes opened like tulips and filled with a spicy cream cheese stuffing, make eye-catching party appetisers.

Sardine and rice parcels

TIP
To prepare each sardine, cut off its head and tail, slit it along the belly, gut it and lay it flat, skin side down. Lift the backbone from the tail end with the knife tip and pull towards the head; all the bones will come away with it.

MAKES 24
PREPARATION TIME: 30 minutes,
plus 15 minutes to cool
COOKING TIME: 10 minutes

2½ oz (70g) long-grain rice
1 tablespoon white wine vinegar
28 large, undamaged spinach leaves
8 small fresh or frozen and thawed sardines, scaled, cleaned, gutted and boned
2 small spring onions, finely chopped
Lemon wedges to garnish
2 level tablespoons English mustard powder mixed with 4 teaspoons water

1   Cook the rice. Mix the vinegar into the rice while it is still warm, then leave the mixture to cool.

2   Meanwhile, spread 4 spinach leaves in a steamer basket and place the sardines on top. Put the basket in the steamer pan over 1in (25mm) of boiling water, cover and steam for about 6 minutes, until the sardines flake readily when tested with a fork. Take the basket out of the steamer and carefully lift the sardines onto a plate. Divide each sardine into three pieces and leave to cool. Discard the spinach.

3   Put the remaining spinach leaves in the steamer basket and steam them for 1 minute. Remove the basket from the steamer, rinse the leaves with cold water and lift them out carefully onto kitchen paper to pat dry.

4   Put a rounded teaspoon of rice at the stem end of a spinach leaf. Set one piece of sardine on top and sprinkle some onion on it. Fold the sides of the leaf over the filling, then roll up to make a neat parcel. Fill the rest of the leaves, arrange the parcels on a serving plate and garnish them with the lemon wedges. Put the mustard beside them to dab on the parcels.

Serve the parcels at once, or cover them and refrigerate for up to 3 hours before serving.

Spinach soufflé squares

MAKES 25 pieces
PREPARATION TIME: 15 minutes
COOKING TIME: 25 minutes
OVEN: Preheat to 200°C (400°F, gas mark 6)

2lb (900g) fresh spinach, trimmed, washed and chopped
⅛ level teaspoon freshly grated nutmeg
8oz (225g) low-fat cottage cheese, drained
2 level teaspoons plain flour
2 level tablespoons grated Parmesan cheese
3 eggs, size 2, separated
⅛ level teaspoon cayenne pepper
Freshly ground black pepper
Red or yellow cherry tomatoes to garnish

1   Put the spinach in a saucepan with only the water that clings to it and sprinkle with the nutmeg. Cook, uncovered, over a moderate heat for about 5 minutes, stirring several times, until the spinach is tender. Drain thoroughly and leave to cool.

2   Blend the cottage cheese in a food processor for 30 seconds or pass it through a nylon sieve. Add the flour, Parmesan, egg yolks, cayenne and black pepper, and blend for a further 30 seconds, or beat with a wooden spoon. Mix with the spinach in a large bowl.

3   Line a baking tin 7½ in (18cm) square with nonstick baking paper.

4   Whisk the egg whites until they hold soft peaks and fold into the spinach mixture, using a large metal spoon. Pour into the tin, smooth the top and bake in the heated oven for about 20 minutes, until set.

5   Cool on a wire rack for 5 minutes, then turn out of the tin, peel off the paper and cut the soufflé into 1½ in (40mm) squares.

Serve at once, garnished with the tomatoes, or cover and refrigerate for up to 24 hours.

Hidden in each of these neat, bite-sized parcels of lightly steamed spinach (right, bottom) is a portion of rice and a morsel of sardine. Spinach is also the vital ingredient in the soufflé squares; there it mingles with cottage cheese, nutmeg and Parmesan to make light, savoury party pieces.

Tomatoes with prawn stuffing

MAKES 24
PREPARATION TIME: 20 minutes,
plus 20 minutes to cool
COOKING TIME: 4 minutes

4oz (115g) raw freshwater prawns
2 level tablespoons chopped fresh parsley
1 clove garlic, peeled and crushed
1 tablespoon lemon juice
1 tablespoon olive oil
1/8 level teaspoon cayenne pepper
24 cherry tomatoes, washed, stalks left on

1   Put the prawns in a saucepan, cover with
unsalted cold water and bring to the boil.
Cook, uncovered, for 2 minutes, or until the
prawns turn pink. Drain and leave for about
20 minutes, until cool enough to handle.

2   Peel and de-vein the prawns
then chop them finely. Mix them in a bowl
with the parsley, garlic, lemon juice, oil
and cayenne pepper. Cover and chill the
mixture in the refrigerator while you are
preparing the tomatoes.

3   Slice the top off each tomato and set aside.
Scoop out the core and seeds carefully with a
small teaspoon and place the shells upside-
down on pieces of kitchen paper until any
liquid has drained out.

4   Fill the tomatoes with the prawn mixture
and place the reserved tops back on them.
Arrange on a serving plate and serve at once or
cover the tomatoes and refrigerate them for
up to 3 hours before serving.

You can use 3oz (85g) of cooked, peeled prawns
in place of the freshwater prawns, but the salt
content will be higher. Use yellow tomatoes,
when you can get them, as well as red ones.

THREE TOMATOES	
CALORIES 32	
TOTAL FAT 2g	
SATURATED FAT 0	
CARBOHYDRATES 2g	
ADDED SUGAR 0	
FIBRE 1g	
SODIUM 15mg	

> **TIP**
> *For the best
> proportion of filling
> to cucumber, use
> thin cucumbers and
> leave a shell about
> 1/2 in (13mm)
> thick. Do not cut
> the slices too thin;
> thicker slices hold
> the filling more
> securely.*

Tuna and cucumber rings

MAKES 30 rings
PREPARATION TIME: 20 minutes,
plus 1–3 hours to refrigerate

3 1/2 oz (100g) tinned tuna in oil, drained
and flaked
1/2 oz (15g) fresh wholemeal breadcrumbs
1 small stick celery, trimmed and finely chopped
2 spring onions, trimmed and finely chopped
4 level tablespoons Greek yoghurt
2 level teaspoons chopped fresh parsley
1 level teaspoon chopped fresh tarragon
2 teaspoons lemon juice
1/2 level teaspoon Dijon mustard
Freshly ground black pepper
1/2 red pepper, de-seeded and finely chopped
2 cucumbers, each about 12oz (340g), washed
Parsley or watercress leaves to garnish

1   Mix the tuna with the breadcrumbs, celery,
onions and yoghurt. Stir in the parsley,
tarragon, lemon juice and mustard, and season
with black pepper. Mix in half the red pepper,
then cover the rest and refrigerate.

2   Trim off the narrow ends of the cucumbers,
then run a cannelle knife or the prongs of a
fork down the length of the cucumbers at
regular intervals to score the skin and give the
cucumbers a green-and-white striped look.
Cut each cucumber into four equal lengths and,
using an apple corer or a small teaspoon,
carefully hollow out the centre of each one.

3   Fill the hollows with the tuna mixture,
pressing it in with a wooden spoon handle. Put
the cucumbers in a dish, cover and refrigerate
for 1 hour for the filling to firm up.

4   Cut the cucumbers into slices about
1/2 in (13mm) thick. Garnish each slice with
a sprinkling of the reserved red pepper and a
parsley or watercress leaf. Arrange the rings
on a plate or tray.

You can prepare and fill the cucumbers up to
3 hours in advance. Keep them covered in the
refrigerator, taking them out and slicing them
30 minutes before serving.

THREE RINGS	
CALORIES 35	
TOTAL FAT 2g	
SATURATED FAT 0	
CARBOHYDRATES 2g	
ADDED SUGAR 0	
FIBRE 0	
SODIUM 55mg	

Rows of brilliant cherry tomatoes filled with prawns, and cucumber rings packed with tuna make a cheerful display for a buffet party.

Banana milk shake

MAKES 4 GLASSES
PREPARATION TIME: 5 minutes

8 ice cubes
1 pint (570ml) semi-skimmed milk
2 large ripe bananas, peeled and sliced
1 teaspoon vanilla extract

1 Blend the ice cubes and milk in a food processor for 1 minute, or until smooth.

2 Add the bananas and vanilla extract and blend for 1 minute more, or until foamy. Pour into tall glasses and serve.

Make this milk shake immediately before serving so that there is no danger that the bananas will discolour. You can also make fruit milk shakes with 8oz (225g) of hulled ripe strawberries or raspberries, adding 2 level teaspoons of caster sugar, if necessary.

Hot chocolate and banana

MAKES 4 CUPS
PREPARATION TIME: 15 minutes

2 level tablespoons cocoa
4 tablespoons cold water
1¼ pints (725ml) skimmed milk
1 vanilla bean, split lengthways
½ level teaspoon ground cinnamon
1 medium, ripe banana, peeled and chopped
2 level tablespoons Greek yoghurt
1 level teaspoon grated plain chocolate

1 Blend the cocoa and water to a paste in a saucepan. Gradually whisk in half the milk.

2 Stir in the vanilla bean and cinnamon and bring to the boil, then simmer for 2-3 minutes, stirring. Discard the vanilla bean.

3 Blend the bananas and remaining milk in a food processor until smooth. Stir into the chocolate milk and bring to the boil.

4 Take off the heat, whisk in the yoghurt, then pour into cups or mugs, and sprinkle with the grated chocolate. Serve immediately.

Milky drinks are wonderfully refreshing when ice-cold and comforting when hot. A summer afternoon is the time for serving tall glasses of iced coffee to the grown-ups and a pale froth of banana milk shake to the children. Young and old alike will enjoy cups of hot chocolate flavoured with banana and vanilla, and given a spicy edge with cinnamon.

Iced coffee

ONE GLASS	
CALORIES	60
TOTAL FAT	1g
SATURATED FAT	0
CARBOHYDRATES	1g
ADDED SUGAR	0
FIBRE	0
SODIUM	105mg

MAKES 4 GLASSES
PREPARATION TIME: 10 minutes

1 level tablespoon cocoa
1 tablespoon cold water
4 level tablespoons ground coffee
6fl oz (175ml) boiling water
1 pint (570ml) skimmed milk, well chilled
½ teaspoon vanilla extract
6 ice cubes

1 Mix the cocoa to a smooth paste in a cup with the cold water.

2 Stir the coffee with the boiling water in a small bowl and leave to stand for 5 minutes.

3 Strain the coffee through a sieve lined with kitchen paper into a blender or food processor. Add the cocoa, milk, vanilla and ice, and blend for 1 minute. Serve at once in tall glasses.

Mulled cider

ONE GLASS

CALORIES 95

TOTAL FAT 0

SATURATED FAT 0

CARBOHYDRATES 8g

ADDED SUGAR 0

FIBRE 0

SODIUM 20mg

MAKES 4 GLASSES
PREPARATION TIME: 10 minutes

1¾ pints (1 litre) dry cider
2 cinnamon sticks, crumbled
8 allspice berries
6 cloves
Thinly pared rind of 1 orange
4 orange wedges

1 Pour the cider into a stainless steel or enamel saucepan, and stir in the crumbled cinnamon sticks, allspice, cloves and orange rind. Bring to the boil, then turn down the heat and leave the cider to simmer, uncovered, for 5 minutes.

2 Strain the hot cider into heatproof glasses and put an orange wedge in each drink.

Bittersweet cider is mellowed by warming and spicing into an aromatic winter beverage for enjoying at the fireside – or round a bonfire.

Shrub is a name borrowed from the Arabs' fruit sherbet drinks. This one is irresistible – deep, glowing pink, ice-cold and refreshingly tart.

Spiced cranberry shrub

ONE GLASS	
CALORIES 45	
TOTAL FAT 0	
SATURATED FAT 0	
CARBOHYDRATES 8g	
ADDED SUGAR 2g	
FIBRE 1g	
SODIUM 5mg	

MAKES 4 GLASSES
PREPARATION TIME: 5 minutes, plus 1 hour to cool

½ pint (285ml) cranberry juice
8fl oz (225ml) dry cider
1 tablespoon cider vinegar
1 cinnamon stick
2 cloves
2 strips lemon rind
12 ice cubes
1 pint (570ml) mineral water, chilled
4 orange slices
Small red-skinned apple

1 Pour the cranberry juice into a stainless steel or enamel saucepan with the cider, vinegar, cinnamon, cloves and lemon rind. Bring to the boil, then take off the heat. Cover and leave for about 1 hour, until cooled.

2 Strain the shrub into a jug and add the ice, mineral water and orange slices. At the last moment slice and add the apple. Serve in chilled glasses.

For a slightly sweeter drink, use half and half cranberry and raspberry juice.

Gingered lemon and lime fizz

TIP
For a frosty appearance, chill the serving glasses in the refrigerator for 1 hour before using.

MAKES 6 GLASSES
PREPARATION TIME: 5 minutes, plus 1 hour to infuse

3 lemons
1 pint (570ml) boiling water
2 level tablespoons peeled and grated root ginger
2oz (60g) sugar
Strained juice of 2 limes
6 slices lemon
6 slices lime
8 ice cubes
1 pint (570ml) soda water or sparkling mineral water, chilled

1 Pare the rind thinly from one lemon. Put the rind into a heatproof jug, pour the boiling water on it and add the ginger and sugar. Stir well, cover and leave to infuse for 1 hour.

2 Squeeze the juice from all three lemons and strain into a serving jug. Add the lime juice, then strain in the liquid from the ginger mixture and stir.

3 Add the lemon and lime slices and the ice to the jug. Top up with the soda water or mineral water. Stir again and serve in tall glasses.

Ginger tea punch

MAKES 10 GLASSES
PREPARATION TIME: 10 minutes, plus 1-2 hours to cool and chill

1½ pints (850ml) boiling water
8 Assam, Darjeeling or Ceylon tea bags
1 level tablespoon caster sugar
3 level tablespoons peeled and grated root ginger, or 1½ level teaspoons ground ginger
1¾ pints (1 litre) soda water or sparkling mineral water
20 ice cubes
Slivers of peeled root ginger for decoration

1 Pour the water into a large heatproof jug and stir in the tea bags, sugar and ginger. Leave the mixture to infuse for 8 minutes, then take out the tea bags. Leave the tea to cool before covering and putting it in the refrigerator for 1-2 hours.

2 Strain the tea through a coffee filter, or a sieve lined with kitchen paper, into a serving jug or punch bowl. Stir in the soda water or mineral water, and serve in long glasses with two ice cubes and a sliver or two of fresh ginger in each glass.

Grapefruit and mint spritzer

MAKES 4 GLASSES
PREPARATION TIME: 10 minutes

Strained juice of two large pink grapefruits
Strained juice of 1 lemon
2 level teaspoons caster sugar
4 sprigs mint
24 ice cubes
½ pint (285ml) soda water or sparkling mineral water, chilled
Mint sprigs for decoration

1 Mix the grapefruit juice with the lemon juice in a jug.

2 Put ½ teaspoon of the sugar and a sprig of mint into each of four glasses. Using the back of a spoon, crush the mint into the sugar.

3 Put 6 ice cubes into each glass and pour in a share of the juice. Top up with the soda water or mineral water. Stir, decorate with mint sprigs and serve.

Drinks are more fun when they gently prickle the palate. The grapefruit spritzer (near right) prickles with sparkling water, while the tea punch and jug of lemon and lime make doubly certain by adding ginger as well.

A steaming glass of this herb tea spreads a tantalising scent of mint, sage and verbena, and makes a thirst-quenching after-dinner drink.

Herb tea

ONE GLASS	
CALORIES	10
TOTAL FAT	0
SATURATED FAT	0
CARBOHYDRATES	3g
ADDED SUGAR	3g
FIBRE	0
SODIUM	0

MAKES 4 GLASSES
PREPARATION TIME: 5 minutes,
plus 5 minutes to infuse

2 level tablespoons dried mint
1 level tablespoon dried sage
1 level tablespoon dried verbena
1¾ pints (1 litre) boiling water
2 teaspoons clear honey
2 teaspoons lemon juice
2 lemon slices, quartered, and fresh sage sprigs
for decoration

1 Spoon the mint, sage and verbena into a large, warmed teapot. Pour on the boiling water and stir quickly, then cover and leave to infuse for 5 minutes.

2 Put ½ teaspoon of honey and ½ teaspoon of lemon juice into each of four tea glasses, then pour in the tea through a strainer. Drop two quarter-slices of lemon into each glass and decorate with a sprig of sage.

You can use thyme or borage instead of verbena.

28

Amber orange-tea punch

MAKES 12 CUPS
PREPARATION TIME: 15 minutes,
plus overnight refrigeration

ONE CUP

CALORIES 40

TOTAL FAT 0

SATURATED FAT 0

CARBOHYDRATES 6g

ADDED SUGAR 0

FIBRE 0

SODIUM 5mg

*An icy cup of spiced
fresh orange juice hisses
gently with the bubbles
of mineral water and
wine. Assam tea gives
the drink perfumed
depths, but devotees of
Earl Grey may prefer
its smoky delicacy.*

4 Assam or Earl Grey tea bags
¾ pint (425ml) boiling water
*¾ pint (425ml) freshly squeezed orange juice
(about 5 large oranges)*
2 cinnamon sticks, cracked
12 cloves
½ pint (285ml) sparkling mineral water, chilled
½ pint (285ml) sparkling dry white wine, chilled
Slices of orange and sprigs of mint for decoration

1 Put the tea bags into a large, heatproof jug,
pour on the boiling water and leave to infuse
for 8 minutes. Remove and discard the tea bags.

2 Pour half the orange juice into a small,
stainless steel or enamel saucepan with the
cinnamon sticks and cloves. Bring to the boil,
then turn down the heat, cover and leave to
simmer for 1 minute.

3 Pour the hot, spiced orange juice into the
jug with the tea, then stir in the remaining
juice. Cover and, when cool enough, put in the
refrigerator and leave overnight.

4 Just before serving, strain the mixture into
a punchbowl and pour in the mineral water
and wine. Float the slices of orange and sprigs
of mint on the punch and serve immediately,
ladling it into silver or glass punch cups, or
into small tumblers.

Orange and pineapple crush

MAKES 4 GLASSES
PREPARATION TIME: 25 minutes

*1 pineapple, about 2lb (900g), sliced, skin, core
and woody eyes removed, flesh chopped*
*½ pint (285ml) freshly squeezed orange juice
(about 4 medium oranges), strained*
2 tablespoons lemon juice, strained
12 ice cubes
½ pint (285ml) soda water or sparkling mineral water
*2 orange slices, halved, and 4 pineapple chunks
for decoration*

1 Blend the pineapple in a food processor for
1-2 minutes, then strain through a nylon sieve,
pressing with a spoon to extract all the juice.
Discard the remaining pulp.

2 Mix the pineapple juice, orange juice and
lemon juice in a jug.

3 Put 3 ice cubes into each of four tall glasses
and pour a share of the fruit juice into each
glass. Top up with the soda water or mineral
water and stir well. Decorate with the halved
orange slices and the pineapple chunks,
threaded on cocktail sticks, and serve at once.

ONE GLASS	
CALORIES 80	
TOTAL FAT 0	
SATURATED FAT 0	
CARBOHYDRATES 20g	
ADDED SUGAR 0	
FIBRE 0	
SODIUM 10mg	

Orange-yoghurt drink

MAKES 4 GLASSES
PREPARATION TIME: 10 minutes

ONE GLASS	
CALORIES 140	
TOTAL FAT 1g	
SATURATED FAT 1g	
CARBOHYDRATES 26g	
ADDED SUGAR 3g	
FIBRE 0	
SODIUM 150mg	

14 oz (400g) low-fat natural yoghurt
¾ pint (425ml) skimmed milk, well chilled
*12fl oz (340ml) freshly squeezed orange juice,
(about 4 large oranges), strained*
2 teaspoons clear honey
½ level teaspoon ground ginger
Orange slices for decoration

1 Blend the yoghurt, milk, orange juice, honey
and ginger in a food processor for 1 minute.

2 Pour into four glasses, decorate with the
orange slices, and serve immediately.

Freshly squeezed orange juice whips to a cool froth with yoghurt (left), and effervesces when mixed with pineapple juice and soda (right).

Passion fruit citrus sodas

ONE GLASS	
CALORIES	25
TOTAL FAT	0
SATURATED FAT	0
CARBOHYDRATES	5g
ADDED SUGAR	3g
FIBRE	0
SODIUM	5mg

MAKES 4 GLASSES
PREPARATION TIME: 20 minutes,
plus 2 hours to cool and chill

Thinly pared rind of 1 gently scrubbed lemon
1/4 pint (150ml) water
2 level teaspoons granulated sugar
10 ripe passion fruits
Strained juice of 1 lemon
Strained juice of 1/2 lime
12 ice cubes
4 thin slices lemon
4 thin slices lime
1 1/2 pints (850ml) soda water, chilled

1 Put the lemon rind, water and sugar into a stainless steel or enamel saucepan. Bring to the boil, stirring to dissolve the sugar, and boil for 1 minute. Remove from the heat and leave to cool for about 30 minutes, then cover and refrigerate for about 1 hour, or until the mixture is very cold.

2 Meanwhile, cut each passion fruit in half and scoop the seeds out with a teaspoon into a nylon sieve placed over a bowl. Rub the seeds firmly in the sieve with the back of a stainless steel spoon to squeeze out all the juice, then discard the seeds.

3 Strain the chilled lemon syrup into the bowl with the passion fruit juice, then strain in the lemon juice and the lime juice and stir the mixture well.

4 Put 3 ice cubes into each of four tall glasses. Ladle a quarter of the fruit juice mixture into each glass and drop a slice of lemon and lime into each one. Top up the glasses with the soda water, stir quickly and serve immediately while still fizzing.

You can prepare the passion fruit and lemon mixture up to 6 hours in advance, if this is more convenient. Cover the bowl and keep it in the refrigerator. Mix it with the ice and soda water just before serving. You can make up the passion fruit mixture into a hot drink; just dilute it with hot water instead of soda water, remembering to use heatproof glasses. Passion fruits can be very tart before they are ripe. If you cannot wait for them to ripen completely, you may need to add a little more sugar.

TIP
Choose passion fruits with wrinkled skin, or keep them until the skin wrinkles. The wrinkling is a sign that the fruit is ripe.

Pineapple-mint yoghurt drink

ONE GLASS	
CALORIES	100
TOTAL FAT	1g
SATURATED FAT	0
CARBOHYDRATES	20g
ADDED SUGAR	3g
FIBRE	0
SODIUM	90mg

MAKES 4 GLASSES
PREPARATION TIME: 10 minutes

1 1/2 lb (680g) fresh pineapple, sliced, skin, core and woody eyes removed, flesh chopped
8oz (225g) low-fat natural yoghurt
8fl oz (225ml) chilled skimmed milk
2 level teaspoons caster sugar
3 level tablespoons chopped fresh mint
Mint sprigs for decoration

1 Put the pineapple flesh with the yoghurt, milk, sugar and chopped mint in a food processor and blend for 1-2 minutes until the mixture has an even, creamy texture.

2 Strain the pineapple drink into four tumblers, decorate each with a mint sprig and serve immediately.

The coolest, palest shade of cream and a heady scent promise smooth and fruity refreshment, a promise that is fulfilled when you taste pineapple-mint yoghurt drink (near right), while the exotic flavours in a jug of passion fruit citrus soda (far right) make a blend just sharp enough to quench the fiercest thirst.

Its warm ruby colour and sharp spicy flavour make this drink popular at outdoor parties — and especially in summer when the evenings can be cool and strings of fruit are hanging on the redcurrant bushes.

TIP
Prepare the redcurrant juice the day before you need it and store in the refrigerator. Or make the juice when redcurrants are in season and freeze it.

Hot redcurrant punch

MAKES 4 CUPS
PREPARATION TIME: 25 minutes

1 pint (570ml) dry cider
1 cinnamon stick, crumbled
4 cloves
4 allspice berries
1 strip of lemon rind
7fl oz (200ml) boiling water
1 tea bag
7fl oz (200ml) redcurrant juice
Redcurrants for decoration

1 Pour the cider into a stainless steel or enamel saucepan. Stir in the cinnamon, cloves, allspice and lemon rind, and bring to the boil. Lower the heat and simmer for 10 minutes.

2 Meanwhile, pour the boiling water on the tea bag in a teapot, cover and leave to infuse for 5 minutes, then discard the tea bag.

3 Pour the tea and the redcurrant juice in with the cider. Heat for 2-3 minutes, until the liquid is hot but not boiling, then strain it into a punchbowl.

4 To serve, ladle the punch into cups or heatproof glasses, and decorate each serving with redcurrants.

ONE CUP

CALORIES 75

TOTAL FAT 0

SATURATED FAT 0

CARBOHYDRATES 9g

ADDED SUGAR 2g

FIBRE 0

SODIUM 10mg

Mixed vegetable juice

MAKES 6 GLASSES
PREPARATION TIME: 10 minutes

8oz (225g) ripe tomatoes, skinned and chopped
2 sticks celery, trimmed and chopped
6oz (175g) cucumber, peeled and sliced
2oz (60g) red pepper, de-seeded and chopped
1 tablespoon lemon juice
1 level teaspoon grated fresh horseradish
3-4 drops Tabasco
4 frozen tomato purée cubes
24 ice cubes
¼ pint (150ml) water
⅛ level teaspoon salt
Celery sticks and cucumber slices to garnish

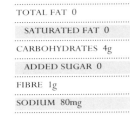

ONE GLASS
....
CALORIES 20
....
TOTAL FAT 0
....
   SATURATED FAT 0
....
CARBOHYDRATES 4g
....
   ADDED SUGAR 0
....
FIBRE 1g
....
SODIUM 80mg
....

1 Put the tomatoes, celery, cucumber and pepper in a liquidiser with the lemon juice, horseradish, Tabasco, tomato purée cubes and 6 of the ice cubes. Add the water and salt, and blend for 2 minutes, until an even texture.

2 Put three ice cubes in each of six glasses and pour in the vegetable juice. Garnish each glass with a celery stick and a cucumber slice and serve immediately.

A cool blend of cucumber and tomato with a hot dash of horseradish makes a long drink in a short time, and each serving has its own swizzle stick of celery.

Crusty breads and rolls

MAKES 2 large loaves, or 4 small loaves,
or 1 large loaf and 18 rolls, or 36 rolls
PREPARATION TIME: About 30 minutes,
plus up to 2 hours to rise
COOKING TIME: 25-40 minutes for loaves,
depending on size; 15 minutes for rolls
OVEN: Preheat to 230°C (450°F, gas mark 8)

½ pint (285ml) lukewarm water
½ level teaspoon caster sugar
2 level tablespoons dried yeast
3lb (1.4kg) plain wholemeal or strong unbleached
plain flour, or a mixture of the two
2 level teaspoons salt
3oz (85g) polyunsaturated margarine
1 pint (570ml) lukewarm skimmed milk

1 Pour the water into a bowl, stir in the sugar
to dissolve it, and whisk in the yeast. Cover and
put in a warm place for 10 minutes until frothy.

2 Sift the flour and salt into a large mixing
bowl, tipping in any bran left in the sieve. Rub
in the margarine and make a well in the centre.

3 Whisk the yeast liquid with the milk, pour
it into the flour and mix to form a soft dough.

4 Knead the dough on a lightly floured surface
by folding it towards you, then pushing it down
and away with the palm of your hand. Give the
dough a quarter turn and repeat. Continue
for about 10 minutes, until the dough is
even-textured, springy and no longer sticky.

5 Put the dough in a clean, lightly floured
bowl and cover with a clean, damp teacloth.
Leave in a warm place (by a radiator or in an
airing cupboard, for example) for 1-1½ hours,
until the dough has doubled in size and
springs back when pressed with a finger.

6 Turn the dough onto a lightly floured work
surface and beat with clenched fists to knock
out the air bubbles. Knead again until
even-textured, then shape into loaves or rolls.

7 For two large tin loaves, grease two
2lb (900g) loaf tins. Divide the dough into two
halves and roll each piece under your hands to
form a smooth roll the same length as the loaf
tin. For four small loaves, divide and shape the
dough to fit 1lb (450g) loaf tins. Fit the dough
into the tins, cover loosely with a clean teacloth
and put in a warm place for about 45 minutes,
or until the dough has risen to the top of the
tins. Make 3 or 4 slashes across the top of each
loaf before baking.

For two large cottage loaves, cut the dough in
half, then cut a third off each piece. Roll the
pieces under your hands to form rounds. Place
the larger rounds on greased baking sheets, and
set the smaller rounds on top. Flour the handle
of a large wooden spoon, push it down through
the centre of each loaf and pull it out again, to
make the pieces join. Cover loosely with clean
teacloths and put in a warm place to rise for
about 1 hour, or until doubled in size.

To make four cob loaves, cut the dough into
quarters. Shape each piece with your hands into
a neat round. Place the loaves well apart on two
greased baking sheets, cover loosely with clean
teacloths and put in a warm place to rise for
about 45 minutes, until doubled in size. Cut a
deep cross in the top of each loaf before baking.

To make two large plaited loaves, cut the dough
in half and cut each half into three equal pieces.
Cover three pieces with an upturned bowl and
roll the others under your hands into strands
18in (46cm) long. Lay the strands together end
on to you and, working from the centre, plait
them towards you, right strand over the centre,
left strand over the new centre, and so on.
Pinch the ends firmly together to seal. Turn the
loaf over and away from you so that the loose
ends are towards you. Plait these in the same
way. Make up the second loaf, then place the
loaves on greased baking sheets and cover
loosely with clean teacloths and put the loaves
in a warm place to rise for about 1 hour, or
until doubled in size.

To make 36 rolls, weigh the dough into
2oz (60g) pieces and roll each one under your
cupped palm into a smooth ball. If you like, you
can then roll out each ball with a rolling pin to
a 3in (85mm) disc to make baps. Alternatively,
you can shape the pieces into mini-plaits or
cottage loaves, or roll them into strands and tie
each into a knot. Place the rolls well apart on
greased baking sheets, cover loosely with clean
teacloths and put in a warm place to rise for
about 45 minutes, or until doubled in size.

ONE ROLL

CALORIES 145

TOTAL FAT 3g

SATURATED FAT 0

CARBOHYDRATES 26g

ADDED SUGAR 0

FIBRE 4g

SODIUM 135mg

TIP
For the lukewarm
water, pour ¼ pint
(150ml) of boiling
water into a
measuring jug, then
add cold water until
the jug feels
comfortably warm
when you touch it
with the inside of
your wrist. Pour off
excess water. The
milk should be
heated until the pan
feels comfortably
warm to your
wrist.

Large or small, plaited, plain or cottage-style, floured, glazed or sprinkled with seeds or oats, homemade crusty loaves and rolls are welcome at any meal from family breakfast to festive dinner party.

8 When the loaves or rolls have risen, and will retain a slight dent if pressed lightly with a fingertip, brush the tops with salty water to give an extra crisp crust. If you prefer a softer crust, leave them plain or dust very lightly with flour. To give the tops a sheen, brush lightly with milk, and for a shiny glaze, brush with an egg beaten with 2 tablespoons of milk. After brushing, you can finish with a sprinkling of poppy seeds, sesame seeds or rolled oats.

9 Bake the bread in the heated oven. Large loaves will take about 40 minutes, small loaves about 25 minutes, and rolls about 15 minutes.

10 Turn the bread over on the baking sheet, or turn out of the tin and rap with a knuckle. It sounds hollow when cooked. If it does not, bake it for a few minutes longer. As soon as the bread is cooked, take it off the baking sheet or out of the tin and put on a wire rack to cool.

Pitta breads

TIP
Be sure to heat the baking sheets thoroughly. This is what makes the pitta breads become hollow in the middle as they cook.

MAKES 10
PREPARATION TIME: 40 minutes,
plus 1 hour 20 minutes to rise
COOKING TIME: 10 minutes
OVEN: Preheat to 240°C (475°F, gas mark 9)

½ pint (285ml) lukewarm water
¼ level teaspoon sugar
2 level teaspoons dried yeast
1lb (450g) strong unbleached plain flour
¼ level teaspoon salt
2 tablespoons olive oil

1 Pour half the water into a bowl, stir in the sugar until it dissolves, then whisk in the yeast. Cover, leave to stand in a warm place for 10 minutes until frothy, then whisk in the rest of the water.

2 Sift the flour and salt into a bowl, make a well in the centre and pour in the yeast liquid and oil. Mix to a soft dough, then knead on a lightly floured surface for about 5 minutes, or until even in texture and springy.

3 Put the dough in a lightly floured bowl and cover with a clean, damp teacloth. Leave in a warm place for 1 hour, or until doubled in size.

4 Turn the dough onto a floured surface and knead for 2 minutes. Divide into 10 equal pieces, shape each into a ball by rolling under your cupped palm, then roll with a rolling pin into very thin ovals about ⅛ in (3mm) thick.

5 Spread out the ovals on two clean, floured teacloths, cover with more teacloths and leave to rise for 20 minutes. Halfway through the rising time, put two lightly greased baking sheets into the heated oven.

6 Quickly put the ovals on the hot baking sheets and bake for about 10 minutes, or until puffed and golden brown. Serve warm.

Very high heat puffs up these Balkan flatbreads, which can then be opened up to provide pockets for filling.

Pretzels with cumin seeds

MAKES 12
PREPARATION TIME: 40 minutes,
plus 1 hour 30 minutes to rise
COOKING TIME: 10 minutes
OVEN: Preheat to 230°C (450°F, gas mark 8)

½ pint (285ml) lukewarm water
¼ level teaspoon caster sugar
2 level teaspoons dried yeast
1lb (450g) strong unbleached plain flour
¼ level teaspoon salt
1oz (30g) polyunsaturated margarine
1 egg, size 3, beaten with 1 teaspoon water
2 level teaspoons cumin seeds

1 Pour half the water into a small bowl and
stir in the sugar until it dissolves. Whisk in the
yeast, cover and leave to stand in a warm place
for 10 minutes, until frothy.

2 Sift the flour and salt into a bowl, rub in the
margarine and make a well in the centre. Mix
the remaining water into the yeast liquid and
pour into the well. Mix to form a soft dough,
then turn onto a lightly floured surface and
knead for about 10 minutes, or until even in
texture, springy and no longer sticky. Put the
dough into a clean, lightly floured bowl, cover
with a clean, damp teacloth and leave in a warm
place for 1 hour, or until doubled in size.

3 Turn the dough onto a floured surface,
knock out the air, then knead for 2 minutes.
Divide the dough into 12 pieces. Take one
piece of the dough for shaping, keeping the rest
covered to prevent them from drying out.

4 To shape a pretzel, roll the dough under
your hands into a sausage shape 20in (50cm)
long. Bring the ends round until they cross
and then take them up to the top of the circle,
spacing them about 1½ in (40mm) apart, and
press in position. Alternatively, roll the ends
of the sausage thinner than the centre and
twist them together before pressing down.
Place on a baking sheet lined with nonstick
baking paper, and cover loosely with a clean
teacloth. Shape the other 11 pretzels in the
same way, cover them loosely and put in a
warm place again for 30 minutes, or until they
have doubled in size.

5 Brush the pretzels with the beaten egg and
sprinkle with cumin seeds. Bake in the heated
oven for about 10 minutes, or until well risen,
golden brown and hollow sounding when
tapped underneath. Cool on wire racks.

For smaller, crisper pretzels, divide the dough
into 24 pieces, roll and curve like horseshoes,
brush with salty water and mark with cuts.

ONE LARGE PRETZEL	
CALORIES	155
TOTAL FAT	3g
SATURATED FAT	0
CARBOHYDRATES	28g
ADDED SUGAR	0
FIBRE	1g
SODIUM	70mg

Cumin gives its distinctive spicy edge to these glossy-topped loose knots of bread.

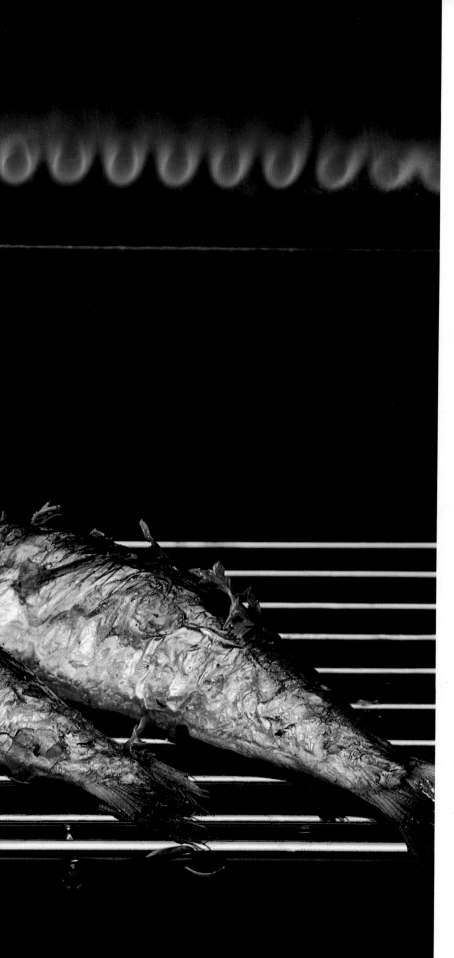

FISH AND SHELLFISH

Quick to cook and easy to digest, fish offers the benefits of animal protein without the overload of saturated fat. The range is wide, from rich pink salmon, to melting mackerel, with prawns and shellfish extending the choice. Sizzling from the grill, chilled in a wine jelly or baked in a paper parcel, they can make healthy family meals and grander dishes for guests.

Soused herrings

SERVES 4
PREPARATION TIME: 20 minutes, plus 1-2 days to marinate
COOKING TIME: 15 minutes
OVEN: Preheat to 180°C (350°F, gas mark 4)

½ pint (285ml) cider vinegar
½ pint (285ml) water
3 juniper berries
6 cloves
¼ level teaspoon ground allspice

6 black peppercorns, lightly crushed
1 bay leaf
4 herrings, each about 8oz (225g), scaled, heads removed, gutted and boned
4 level teaspoons English mustard powder
2 teaspoons water
2 small red onions, peeled, thinly sliced and separated into rings
1 level tablespoon pickled capers, drained
2 small dill-pickled cucumbers, halved lengthways
Wooden cocktail sticks

Richly spiced and sharpened by the mustard and capers, these plump, home-pickled herrings re-create a traditional Scandinavian delicacy.

1 Bring the vinegar, water, juniper berries, cloves, allspice, peppercorns and bay leaf to the boil in a stainless steel or enamel pan, then simmer, uncovered, for 10 minutes. Set aside.

2 Rinse the herrings, pat them dry with kitchen paper and lay them, skin side down, on a board covered with greaseproof paper. Mix the mustard with the water, spread a quarter of the mixture on each fish and arrange a few onion rings and capers on top. Lay a piece of pickled cucumber across the head end of each fillet, and roll up from head to tail. Secure each roll with a cocktail stick.

3 Pack the herrings snugly into an ovenproof glass or china dish and scatter the remaining onion rings on top. Pour the spiced vinegar over the fish. Cover the dish and bake in the heated oven for about 15 minutes, or until the flesh just begins to flake when tested with the tip of a knife. Leave to cool.

4 Remove the cocktail sticks and put the covered dish of herrings in the refrigerator for 1-2 days to 'souse'.

Potato salad, crisp lamb's lettuce and tomatoes are foils for the sharp taste of the herrings.

Fisherman's mackerel

SERVES 4
PREPARATION TIME: 5 minutes
COOKING TIME: 15 minutes

8 mackerel fillets, each about 4oz (115g)
Freshly ground black pepper
2 tablespoons lemon juice
Sprigs of fresh dill and lemon wedges to garnish

1 Rinse the mackerel and pat dry with kitchen paper. Season on both sides with pepper.

2 Line the grill pan with foil. Arrange the opened mackerel skin side down on the grill rack. Grill under a moderate heat without turning for 10-15 minutes, according to their thickness. The flesh should flake easily and be very slightly browned; do not overcook or the fish will be dry.

3 Turn the mackerel over one by one onto a warmed plate, peel off the skins, then arrange them, grilled side up, on a warmed serving dish and sprinkle with the lemon juice. Garnish with the sprigs of dill and lemon wedges.

ONE SERVING	
CALORIES	335
TOTAL FAT	27g
SATURATED FAT	5g
CARBOHYDRATES	0
ADDED SUGAR	0
FIBRE	0
SODIUM	215mg

Fresh mackerel fillets are often overlooked in favour of smoked – a pity, since they are quick to cook and satisfyingly rich to eat because of the oils they contain.

Salmon with cucumber and dill sauce

ONE SERVING	
CALORIES	245
TOTAL FAT	15g
SATURATED FAT	3g
CARBOHYDRATES	3g
ADDED SUGAR	0
FIBRE	0
SODIUM	165mg

SERVES 6
PREPARATION TIME: 10 minutes
COOKING TIME: 25 minutes
OVEN: Preheat to 180°C (350°F, gas mark 4)

2lb (900g) middle-cut or tail-end salmon
in one piece
1 small cucumber, peeled, de-seeded and diced
4oz (115g) low-fat natural yoghurt

2 level teaspoons coarsely chopped fresh
dill, or ½ teaspoon dill seeds
1 teaspoon skimmed milk or water
½ level teaspoon made English mustard
Freshly ground white or black pepper
Thinly sliced cucumber and chopped fresh dill
to garnish

1 Lay the salmon in a baking dish lined with
a large piece of foil. Pour in cold water to a
depth of about ½ in (13mm), then bring all the
sides of the foil together to enclose the salmon
and water. Cook in the heated oven for about
25 minutes, or until the salmon is opaque
and flakes easily.

2 Meanwhile, combine the diced cucumber,
yoghurt, chopped dill or dill seeds, milk or
water and mustard, and season with pepper.
Cover the sauce and put in the refrigerator.

3 Unwrap the salmon, lift it carefully onto a
serving plate and remove the skin. Cut into the
fish horizontally along the sides as far as the
spine, and lift off the upper part of the flesh.
Remove the bones and replace the flesh.

Garnish the salmon with cucumber slices and
dill, and serve it warm or cold with the sauce.
New potatoes or wholemeal bread, and a leafy
salad are simple foils for this summer treat.

*Dill gives the sauce a warm, sweet taste similar to
caraway. Combined with the freshness of cucumber, it
makes a perfect complement to the rich salmon.*

Salmon fish cakes

ONE SERVING	
CALORIES	360
TOTAL FAT	17g
SATURATED FAT	3g
CARBOHYDRATES	29g
ADDED SUGAR	0
FIBRE	3g
SODIUM	240mg

SERVES 4
PREPARATION TIME: 30 minutes
COOKING TIME: 10 minutes

11oz (300g) potatoes, peeled
12oz (340g) salmon steaks
2 level tablespoons low-fat natural yoghurt
1 beaten egg, size 2
1 medium carrot, peeled and finely grated

1 large onion, peeled and finely chopped
½ level teaspoon paprika
1 teaspoon lemon juice
2oz (60g) fine wholemeal breadcrumbs
1½ tablespoons corn oil
Lemon wedges and chervil sprigs to garnish

1 Put the potatoes in boiling water and cook
for 8-10 minutes, until tender.

2 Meanwhile, line the grill pan with foil, lay the salmon steaks on the rack and grill for 2-3 minutes on each side, until opaque all through. Skin and bone the steaks and flake the flesh.

3 Mash the potatoes without milk or fat. Turn them into a bowl and mix in the salmon, yoghurt, egg, carrot, onion, paprika and lemon juice. Divide the mixture into eight and shape each piece into a flat cake.

4 Spread the crumbs on a plate and lay two or three cakes at a time on it. Use a spoon and palette knife to press crumbs gently onto the top and sides of the cakes.

5 Heat the oil in a large nonstick frying pan and fry the fish cakes in it over a moderate heat for 3 minutes on each side, until golden brown.

Serve the salmon fish cakes garnished with the lemon wedges and chervil. A mixed leafy salad makes a fittingly crisp accompaniment. Instead of making the cakes with salmon, you can use 7oz (200g) of tinned tuna, drained of oil.

Soft pink salmon inside a crust of crisp golden crumbs makes fish cakes that are the focus of a filling meal. Although substantial, the cakes are surprisingly light and go well with salads.

> **TIP**
> *To make the salmon cakes easier to shape and coat, prepare the mixture early and put it in the refrigerator for an hour to chill.*

Grating horseradish for the sauce may bring tears to your eyes, but it gives an unmistakable piquancy to this simple dish of grilled salmon.

Grilled salmon with horseradish sauce

SERVES 4
PREPARATION TIME: 5 minutes
COOKING TIME: 5 minutes

5oz (150g) Greek yoghurt
5oz (150g) low-fat natural yoghurt
3 spring onions, trimmed and chopped
10 radishes, washed and chopped
3 level tablespoons freshly grated horseradish
½ level teaspoon ground cumin
Freshly ground black pepper
1 tablespoon olive oil
4 salmon steaks, each about 4oz (115g)
1 tablespoon lemon juice

1 To make the sauce, mix the yoghurts, onions, radishes, horseradish, cumin and pepper in a bowl. Cover and refrigerate.

2 Line the grill pan with foil, oil the rack and heat the grill. Rinse and dry the salmon and lay on the rack. Mix the remaining oil with the lemon juice, season with pepper and trickle half the mixture over the steaks. Cook under a medium grill for 2-3 minutes, until lightly browned. Turn the steaks over, trickle the remaining oil mixture over them and grill for a further 2-3 minutes, or until the steaks are opaque right through the centre.

Serve the salmon on warmed plates with a spoonful of the chilled sauce beside each steak. Saffron-tinted rice and steamed courgettes are perfect foils for the rich salmon. If you cannot find fresh horseradish, use 1 level tablespoon of Dijon mustard in the sauce instead, but it will have less character.

Lemon-marinated sardines

SERVES 4
PREPARATION TIME: 20 minutes,
plus 30 minutes to marinate
COOKING TIME: 8 minutes

1 tablespoon olive oil
Juice of 1 lemon
1 clove garlic, peeled and crushed
2 level tablespoons chopped fresh parsley
Freshly ground black pepper
2lb (900g) fresh sardines, scaled and gutted,
washed and dried with kitchen paper
Lemon wedges and parsley sprigs to garnish

1 Mix the oil, lemon juice, garlic and chopped parsley in a wide dish and season with pepper. Turn the fish in the mixture until coated, then cover and leave to marinate for 30 minutes.

2 Line the grill pan with foil and lay the fish on the rack. Cook under a hot grill for about 8 minutes, turning once. Baste frequently with the marinade. Lift the fish carefully onto a warmed serving dish, pour on the juices and garnish with lemon wedges and parsley sprigs.

ONE SERVING

CALORIES 220

TOTAL FAT 12g

SATURATED FAT 2g

CARBOHYDRATES 0

ADDED SUGAR 0

FIBRE 0

SODIUM 135mg

Fresh sardines are popular in many southern European countries, where they are usually grilled or barbecued. In this recipe, a marinade containing plenty of lemon juice balances the richness of the fish.

Exploit the versatility of tinned tuna by combining it with Indian spices and a mixture of juicy fruits to create this refreshing summer dish.

Curried tuna and fruit

SERVES 4
PREPARATION TIME: 20 minutes, plus 1 hour to chill

4oz (115g) low-fat natural yoghurt
1 level tablespoon mild curry powder
¼ level teaspoon each ground cumin, ground
cardamom and coriander
14oz (400g) tinned tuna, drained of oil, flaked
1 large orange, peel and pith pared off, segments
cut free of membranes and each divided into three
5oz (150g) fresh pineapple, cut into chunks
3oz (85g) each red and green seedless grapes, halved
4oz (115g) water chestnuts, sliced
12 cos lettuce leaves, washed and dried

1 Mix the yoghurt, curry powder, cumin, cardamom and coriander in a large bowl.

2 Gently mix in the tuna, orange, pineapple, grapes and water chestnuts until coated with dressing. Chill in the refrigerator for 1 hour.

3 Arrange the lettuce leaves on individual plates and spoon the tuna and fruit on top.

Serve with crusty rolls or brown rice dressed with lemon juice. You may prefer to peel the grapes and use well-drained unsweetened tinned pineapple in place of fresh.

ONE SERVING	
CALORIES	290
TOTAL FAT	10g
SATURATED FAT	2g
CARBOHYDRATES	22g
ADDED SUGAR	0
FIBRE	3g
SODIUM	340mg

Devilled crab

SERVES 4
PREPARATION TIME: 30 minutes
COOKING TIME: 15 minutes

1oz (30g) polyunsaturated margarine
3 medium spring onions, trimmed and
finely chopped
1 medium stick celery, trimmed and finely chopped
1 level tablespoon plain flour
¼ pint (150ml) skimmed milk
1 level teaspoon Dijon mustard
1 teaspoon lemon juice
¼ level teaspoon cayenne pepper
1lb (450g) cooked fresh crabmeat, white and
brown, roughly chopped
1 level tablespoon chopped fresh parsley
4 level tablespoons dry breadcrumbs

1   Melt half the margarine in a saucepan and
cook the spring onions and celery in it over a
moderate heat for about 5 minutes, until they
are just beginning to soften but not browned.
Blend in the flour and cook for 1 minute.
Gradually stir in the milk and bring to the boil,
stirring continuously, until the sauce is thick
and smooth. Simmer for 2 minutes.

2   Remove the sauce from the heat and
blend in the mustard, lemon juice and cayenne
pepper. Stir in the crabmeat and parsley, and
reheat the sauce to simmering point.

3   Melt the remaining margarine in a small
saucepan without letting it colour, and stir in
the breadcrumbs.

4   Divide the crab mixture between four
scallop shells or individual gratin dishes.
Sprinkle a quarter of the butter and crumb
mixture over the top of each.

5   Cook under a hot grill for 3-4 minutes,
until bubbling hot and golden brown on top,
and serve immediately.

*The crunchy vegetables and breadcrumb topping
offer a contrast in texture to the soft crabmeat,
while the parsley and spices add a peppery spark.*

A pasta salad or crusty bread and a leafy salad
will go well with this dish. In place of the fresh
crab you can use tinned crab, well drained, or
frozen crabmeat completely thawed.

ONE SERVING	
CALORIES 235	
TOTAL FAT 8g	
SATURATED FAT 1g	
CARBOHYDRATES 10g	
ADDED SUGAR 0	
FIBRE 0	
SODIUM 610mg	

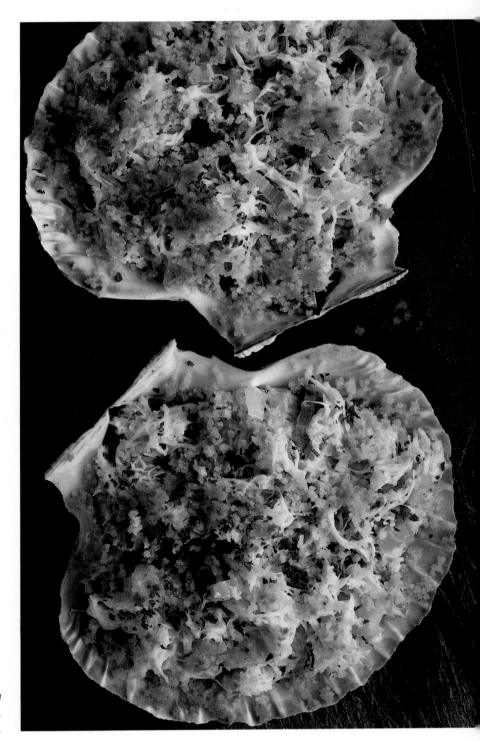

Spiced prawns

SERVES 4
PREPARATION TIME: 20 minutes, plus 4 hours
to refrigerate
COOKING TIME: 10 minutes

2 tablespoons olive oil
1½ lb (680g) frozen, uncooked freshwater prawns,
thawed, peeled and de-veined
2 spring onions, trimmed, green part finely sliced,
white part chopped
2 level teaspoons peeled and grated root ginger,
or ¼ level teaspoon ground ginger
¼ pint (150ml) fish stock
2 tablespoons tomato purée
2 tablespoons dry sherry
2 tablespoons cider vinegar
¼ level teaspoon cayenne pepper
8 cos lettuce leaves, washed and patted dry

ONE SERVING	
CALORIES	140
TOTAL FAT	8g
SATURATED FAT	1g
CARBOHYDRATES	1g
ADDED SUGAR	0
FIBRE	0
SODIUM	175mg

1 Heat half the oil in a frying pan and stir-fry
the prawns in it over a moderate heat for
2 minutes. Spoon into a dish.

2 Heat the remaining oil in the pan, and
stir-fry the white onion and ginger for
30 seconds. Stir in the stock, tomato
purée, sherry, vinegar and cayenne pepper.
Simmer for 3 minutes.

3 Return the prawns to the pan and cook for
3 minutes, stirring. Add half the green onion
and pour the prawns and sauce into a bowl.
Cool, then cover and refrigerate for 4 hours.

4 Arrange the lettuce on four plates, spoon in
the prawns and scatter on the remaining onion.

Serve with brown rice and lamb's lettuce.
You can use cooked and peeled North Atlantic
prawns but their salt content is much higher.

*Crisp lettuce leaves hold cool
prawns, but in the sherry sauce
there are sparks of fire, given by
ginger and cayenne pepper.*

Plaice and vegetable parcels

ONE SERVING

CALORIES 195

TOTAL FAT 9g

SATURATED FAT 2g

CARBOHYDRATES 2g

ADDED SUGAR 0

FIBRE 1g

SODIUM 230mg

SERVES 4
PREPARATION TIME: 15 minutes
COOKING TIME: 10 minutes
OVEN: Preheat to 200°C (400°F, gas mark 6)

1 rounded teaspoon finely snipped fresh chives
1 teaspoon lemon juice
½ level teaspoon paprika
1oz (30g) polyunsaturated margarine

1 small red pepper, de-seeded and thinly sliced
2 large spring onions, trimmed and sliced diagonally
4oz (115g) thin asparagus, trimmed and sliced diagonally
1 small courgette, trimmed and thinly sliced diagonally
4 plaice double fillets, each about 5oz (150g), skinned
4 thin slices lemon

Tender white plaice and crisp, colourful vegetables mingle their juices while cooking and release strong, fresh aromas as the steaming parcels are unwrapped.

1 Work the chives, lemon juice and paprika into the margarine with a knife and set aside.

2 Boil the vegetables for 1 minute in just enough water to cover. Drain and set aside.

3 Cut 4 pieces of nonstick baking paper, each large enough to enclose one plaice fillet. Lay a fillet on each sheet, skinned side down. Spoon a quarter of the vegetables onto each fillet and top the vegetables with a quarter of the chive mixture and a slice of lemon. Fold the edges of the baking paper together over the fish and fold the ends over before tucking them beneath the fish to make secure parcels.

4 Lift the parcels carefully into a baking dish and cook in the heated oven for 10 minutes.

Serve the parcels for the diners to open. Crusty bread and a leafy salad go well with the plaice in summer, while baked garlic potatoes make a satisfying winter accompaniment. You can use sole or flounder instead of plaice.

BEEF, LAMB AND PORK

Red meat is invaluable for the complete protein, vitamins and minerals it contributes to the diet, but these go hand in hand with the saturated fats that should be avoided. The knack is to make a little meat go a long way, and these recipes show how to do it. They skilfully use prudent portions in delicious dishes, cooked by roasting and stewing and by quick grilling and stir-frying to cut down fat but keep flavour intact.

Beefburgers Scandinavian style

SERVES 4
PREPARATION TIME: 10 minutes, plus 20 minutes
to chill
COOKING TIME: 15 minutes

12oz (340g) beef with fat removed, minced
3oz (85g) cooked beetroot, peeled and diced
2oz (60g) fresh wholemeal breadcrumbs

1 egg, size 3, beaten
2 teaspoons red wine vinegar
½ level teaspoon dried dill
Freshly ground black pepper
1 tablespoon olive oil
Shredded lettuce, onion rings and dill fronds
to garnish
Soured cream to garnish

1 Combine the beef, beetroot, breadcrumbs, egg, vinegar and dried dill, and season with pepper. Divide the mixture into four, shape into flat cakes and refrigerate for 20 minutes.

2 Heat the oil in a frying pan and brown the beefburgers over a high heat for 1-2 minutes on each side. Lower the heat to moderate and cook the burgers for 5 minutes more on each side.

3 Drain the beefburgers on kitchen paper before arranging them on individual plates and garnishing with the lettuce, onion and dill. Hand the soured cream round for the diners to put a teaspoonful on their burger; you can mix a little chopped dill with the cream.

Serve the burgers with warm rolls and side salads of cucumber, apple and lettuce.

Beetroot gives the beefburgers a rich colour and a hint of sweetness which is offset by soured cream in a favourite Scandinavian combination.

Beef wrapped in cabbage leaves

SERVES 4
PREPARATION TIME: 40 minutes
COOKING TIME: 25 minutes
OVEN: Preheat to 200°C (400°F, gas mark 6)

1 tablespoon olive oil
1 large clove garlic, peeled and crushed
1 small red onion, peeled and finely chopped
2 rashers unsmoked back bacon, trimmed of fat and chopped
1lb (450g) beef with fat removed, minced
Sprig fresh oregano

3 basil leaves, chopped, or ¼ level teaspoon dried basil
¼ level teaspoon freshly grated nutmeg or ground nutmeg
Freshly ground black pepper
1 level teaspoon arrowroot
1 tablespoon balsamic vinegar
3fl oz (85ml) unsweetened red grape juice
14oz (400g) tinned chopped tomatoes
8 large savoy cabbage leaves
8oz (225g) cooked borlotti or black-eyed beans

1 Heat the oil in a large frying pan and toss the garlic and onion in it over a high heat for 1 minute. Add the bacon and cook for 1 minute. Stir in the beef and fry for about 10 minutes until brown, breaking up any lumps that form. Stir in the oregano, basil and nutmeg, and season with pepper.

2 Blend the arrowroot with the vinegar and grape juice and stir into the minced-beef mixture until the juices come to the boil and thicken. Pour in the tomatoes and simmer, covered, for 20 minutes.

3 Meanwhile bring a large saucepan of water to the boil and cook the cabbage for 2 minutes, then rinse with cold water and drain.

4 Mix the beans into the beef thoroughly, then turn the mixture into a sieve set over a bowl and discard the oregano. Let the juices drain out and keep them for the sauce.

5 Lay the cabbage leaves inside up on a board. Spoon the beef mixture onto the leaves, fold the sides in over the filling and roll the leaves up firmly. Arrange the rolls, seam side down, in one layer in a casserole. Add 2-3 tablespoons of water, put on the lid and bake in the heated oven for about 20 minutes, or until the leaf ribs are just tender.

6 Bring the reserved juices to the boil in a small saucepan while you lift the cabbage rolls onto a heated serving dish. Pour the sauce round them.

A tomato gratin and mashed potato with swede add colour and varied texture to the parcels of beef and beans.

Deep green, crinkly leaves of the savoy cabbage make attractive, crisp wrappings for a substantial, well-flavoured beef and bean filling.

Beef parcels with chestnuts and red wine

SERVES 4
PREPARATION TIME: 30 minutes
COOKING TIME: 1 hour
OVEN: Preheat to 160°C (325°F, gas mark 3)

4oz (115g) chestnuts, shell and inner skin removed,
finely chopped
2oz (60g) mushrooms, wiped and finely chopped
1 small carrot, peeled and grated
1 clove garlic, peeled and crushed
1 level tablespoon whole-grain mustard
2 level teaspoons chopped fresh thyme
⅛ level teaspoon salt
Freshly ground black pepper
4 slices braising beef, each about 4oz (115g),
fat removed, beaten out thin
Thin string to tie parcels
1 tablespoon olive oil
3 shallots or small onions, peeled and finely sliced
1 level tablespoon plain flour
¼ pint (150ml) red wine
¼ pint (150ml) vegetable or beef stock

1 Mix together thoroughly the chestnuts,
mushrooms, carrot, garlic, mustard, thyme and
salt, and season with pepper. Spread out the
beef slices on a board and spoon a quarter of
the chestnut mixture onto the centre of each.
Wrap the meat round the stuffing to make four
neat parcels and tie with clean, thin string.

2 Heat the oil in a flameproof casserole and
brown the parcels in it over a high heat. Lift
them out with a slotted spoon and set aside.
Cook the shallots or onions in the casserole
gently for 2-3 minutes. Stir in the flour and
cook for 1 minute, then gradually stir in the
wine and stock and continue stirring while the
sauce comes to the boil and thickens.

3 Return the beef parcels to the casserole,
cover and cook in the heated oven for 1 hour.
Carefully snip and remove the string when
you serve the parcels.

Cauliflower, baked tomatoes and jacket
potatoes go well with the moist beef parcels.
You can use ale in place of the wine and, when
chestnuts are out of season, soaked and
chopped dried chestnuts can replace them.
If you gather your own chestnuts, be sure they
are sweet chestnuts, not horse chestnuts.

ONE SERVING	
CALORIES	275
TOTAL FAT	10g
SATURATED FAT	3g
CARBOHYDRATES	16g
ADDED SUGAR	0
FIBRE	2g
SODIUM	140mg

TIP
Chestnuts peel
easily if you cut a
deep cross in the top
of each, put them in
a pan with cold
water to cover,
bring to the boil
and simmer for
10 minutes. Spoon
out one at a time
to peel.

*The sweet chestnut
stuffing and the rich
wine sauce are delicious
accompaniments to the
thinly beaten slices of
beef. They combine to
make an unusual
autumn dish.*

Beef kebabs with courgettes and tomatoes

SERVES 4
PREPARATION TIME: 20 minutes, plus 3 hours
to marinate
COOKING TIME: 15 minutes

4 level tablespoons low-fat natural yoghurt
2 tablespoons lemon juice
2 cloves garlic, peeled and finely chopped
2 level teaspoons peeled and grated root ginger,
or ½ level teaspoon ground ginger
2 level teaspoons paprika
½ level teaspoon each cayenne pepper, ground
nutmeg, cumin and coriander
1lb (450g) rump steak with fat removed,
cut into 12 cubes
1 medium courgette, trimmed and cut into 12 slices
1 large red pepper, de-seeded and cut
into 12 squares
4 long metal skewers
8 cherry tomatoes
2 small onions, peeled and cut into quarters
Fresh coriander leaves to garnish

1 Mix the yoghurt, lemon juice, garlic and
ginger with the paprika, cayenne pepper,
nutmeg, cumin and coriander. Whisk the
mixture well, or blend it in a food processor
for 10 seconds.

2 Pour the mixture into a glass or china bowl
and turn the beef cubes in it to coat well. Cover
and put in the refrigerator for 3 hours to
marinate. Turn the meat once during this time.

3 Blanch the courgette and pepper for one
minute in boiling water.

4 Lift the beef cubes out of the marinade and
thread onto four oiled skewers, with a share of
the courgette, red pepper, tomatoes and onion.
Lay the kebabs on the grill rack and cook under
a high heat for 15-20 minutes, frequently
brushing with the marinade and turning until
the meat and vegetables are tender. Reduce the
heat if the kebabs are browning too much.

Serve the kebabs very hot, still on their skewers,
on a bed of boiled green lentils and garnished
with fresh coriander. A dish of diced cucumber
mixed with low-fat natural yoghurt is a
welcome cool accompaniment to the spicy
kebabs. For a summer meal, you might prefer
rolls and a leafy salad with the kebabs.

ONE SERVING	
CALORIES	185
TOTAL FAT	6g
SATURATED FAT	3g
CARBOHYDRATES	8g
ADDED SUGAR	0
FIBRE	1g
SODIUM	90mg

*Marinating meat in yoghurt and lemon juice makes
it a fittingly tender partner for the vegetables in this
colourful dish. Here the yoghurt is warmly spiced.*

Lamb curry

TIP
You will find it quicker to brown the cubes of lamb a few at a time so the heat in the pan remains high.

SERVES 4
PREPARATION TIME: 25 minutes
COOKING TIME: 55 minutes

1 tablespoon corn oil
1lb (450g) meat from boned chump ends or neck fillet of lamb, fat removed, cut into small cubes
1 medium onion, peeled and thinly sliced
½ small stick celery, trimmed and thinly sliced
1 clove garlic, peeled and crushed
1-2 level tablespoons curry powder
½ level teaspoon each ground cumin, ground cardamom and ground coriander
1 small carrot, peeled and grated
4fl oz (115ml) beef stock
¼ level teaspoon cayenne pepper
1 cooking apple, unpeeled, cored and cut into cubes
8oz (225g) small okra or fine green beans, trimmed
2oz (60g) raisins
4oz (115g) low-fat natural yoghurt

1 Heat the oil in a large, heavy-based frying pan and brown the lamb cubes in it on all sides over a high heat. Use a slotted spoon to lift the meat out and put it to drain on kitchen paper.

2 Cook the onion, celery and garlic gently in the frying pan for 5 minutes, stirring frequently. Add the curry powder, cumin, cardamom and coriander and stir for 1 minute. Stir in the lamb, carrot, stock or water and cayenne pepper. Cover and simmer for 40 minutes, or until the lamb is tender.

3 Mix in the apple, okra or beans, and raisins, and a little water if necessary. Cover and cook for 5 minutes, or until the okra is tender.

4 Blend in the yoghurt and heat, taking care not to boil or it will curdle.

Brown or basmati rice and a side dish of thinly sliced tomatoes and onion rings, or coarsely grated carrots would go well with the curry. You can add a garnish of parsley or coriander sprigs for a fresh touch of colour.

Raisins accentuate the tender sweetness of the lamb, striking a perfect balance with the hot, savoury curry spices and sharp, crisp apple.

Herbed lamb cutlets

SERVES 4
PREPARATION TIME: 5 minutes
COOKING TIME: 8 minutes

8 lamb cutlets, each about 4oz (115g), fat trimmed
2 cloves garlic, peeled and halved
1 tablespoon olive oil
1 level tablespoon chopped mixed fresh thyme,
marjoram and rosemary, or 1 level teaspoon dried
mixed herbs
Freshly ground black pepper
Fresh mint and lemon wedges to garnish

1 Lay the cutlets in a shallow dish and rub all over with the cut side of the garlic cloves. Brush both sides of the cutlets with the oil, coat with the herbs and season with pepper.

2 Place the cutlets on the grill rack and cook under a high heat for 4 minutes on each side. Arrange them on warmed serving plates and garnish with the mint and lemon.

Serve with new potatoes and a green salad, and let the diners remove any remaining fat.

TIP
To enhance the herb flavour of the cutlets, coat them 4-5 hours before cooking, cover the dish and put in the refrigerator to marinate.

For ease of preparation and freshness of taste, nothing beats young and tender lamb cutlets briefly grilled in a coating of lively herbs.

Stuffed leg of lamb with orange sauce

SERVES 8
PREPARATION TIME: 25 minutes
COOKING TIME: 2 hours 30 minutes-3 hours
OVEN: Preheat to 230°C (450°F, gas mark 8)

1 tablespoon olive oil
1 large onion, peeled and finely chopped
4 cloves garlic, peeled and crushed
1lb (450g) button mushrooms, wiped and chopped
2oz (60g) wholemeal bread with
crusts cut off, diced
1oz (30g) fresh parsley, finely chopped
1 level teaspoon dried marjoram
½ level teaspoon dried basil
1 medium orange
Freshly ground black pepper
6lb (2.7kg) leg of lamb, bone and fat removed
1 level tablespoon plain flour
½ pint (285ml) vegetable or beef stock
Orange wedges and sprigs of marjoram to garnish

1 Heat the oil in a large frying pan and cook the onion and garlic in it gently for 5 minutes, until lightly coloured. Add the mushrooms and cook for a further 8 minutes, or until the mushroom juices have evaporated.

2 Take the pan off the heat and mix in the bread, parsley, marjoram and basil. Grate in about 1 teaspoon of rind from the orange, season with pepper and stir well.

3 Stuff the lamb with the mushroom mixture, packing the stuffing, not too tightly, along the cavity left by removing the bone. Secure with skewers or thin, clean string if necessary to hold the meat in shape.

4 Put the lamb on a rack in a shallow roasting tin and roast in the heated oven, uncovered, for 15 minutes. Reduce the oven temperature to 180°C (350°F, gas mark 4), and continue cooking for another 2 hours for meat that is slightly pink and 2 hours 20 minutes for well-done meat.

5 Pare off the skin and outer membrane of the orange with a very sharp knife. Free the segments by cutting down each side of them to remove the membranes.

6 When the lamb is cooked, lift it onto a warmed serving dish, cover with foil and leave to rest for 10 minutes. Skim off and discard the fat from the juices in the roasting tin. Mix the flour into the remaining juices and gradually stir in the stock. Bring to the boil over a low heat, stirring to incorporate the browned juices from the bottom of the tin. Reduce the heat and simmer for 5 minutes, stirring frequently. Add the orange segments and heat through for 1 minute, then pour into a heated sauceboat.

7 Uncover the lamb and remove any skewers and string. Slice the meat, not too thinly, leaving the diners to remove any remaining fat. Garnish with the orange wedges and marjoram. Serve with the sauce.

The traditional accompaniments of new potatoes and peas cannot be bettered, but you can offer a different look with mangetout or sugar snap peas.

ONE SERVING
CALORIES 335
TOTAL FAT 18g
SATURATED FAT 7g
CARBOHYDRATES 7g
ADDED SUGAR 0
FIBRE 2g
SODIUM 285mg

TIP
Push the stuffing into the leg cavity with a wooden spoon, using the handle end if necessary to reach the centre.

A mushroom stuffing, seasoned with onion, garlic and herbs, and a sauce infused with orange juice and zest, moisten the meat and sharpen the mild flavour of the roast lamb. The leg, a popular cut, provides plenty of tender, lean meat, delicious hot or cold.

Indonesian-style pork kebabs

SERVES 4
PREPARATION TIME: 20 minutes, plus 1 hour
to marinate
COOKING TIME: 20 minutes

½ level teaspoon ground ginger
2 cloves garlic, peeled
1 small onion, peeled and chopped
1 teaspoon soy sauce
2 level tablespoons unsalted peanuts, toasted
1 teaspoon olive oil
2 level teaspoons soft brown sugar

2 teaspoons lemon juice
½ level teaspoon each ground coriander, cumin
and cinnamon
2 tablespoons water
12oz (340g) pork tenderloin, trimmed of fat and
cut into cubes
4 metal or wooden skewers
Finely shredded lemon rind, spring onion and
parsley leaves to garnish

ONE SERVING

CALORIES	205
TOTAL FAT	11g
SATURATED FAT	2g
CARBOHYDRATES	5g
ADDED SUGAR	3g
FIBRE	1g
SODIUM	160mg

1 Put the ginger, garlic, onion, soy sauce, peanuts, oil, sugar, lemon juice, coriander, cumin and cinnamon in a food processor with the water. Blend for 8-10 seconds, until smooth, then pour into a glass or china dish. Stir the pork cubes into the mixture, cover and put in the refrigerator to marinate for 1 hour.

2 Thread the meat onto the skewers, ensuring that the cubes do not touch one another.

3 Lay the kebabs on a grill rack and brush them with the marinade. Grill for about 20 minutes under a high heat, turning and brushing with the marinade several times, until the pork is cooked through. Arrange the kebabs on a heated serving dish and garnish with the lemon rind, spring onion and parsley.

Boiled rice provides a simple base for the richly flavoured meat, and a crunchy bean sprout and pepper salad refreshes the palate.

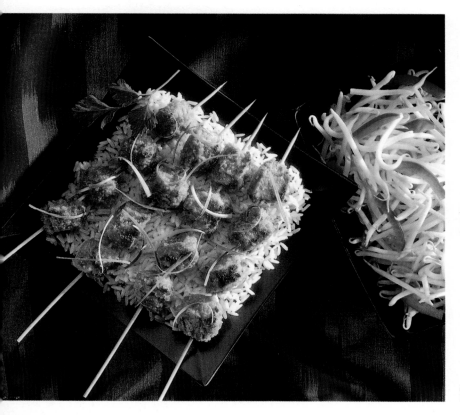

The spicy peanut marinade gives an exotic taste of the East to beautifully tender morsels of pork grilled on skewers to brown every side to perfection.

Stuffed loin of pork

ONE SERVING

CALORIES	345
TOTAL FAT	14g
SATURATED FAT	4g
CARBOHYDRATES	12g
ADDED SUGAR	0
FIBRE	2g
SODIUM	185mg

SERVES 4
PREPARATION TIME: 25 minutes
COOKING TIME: 45 minutes
OVEN: Preheat to 200°C (400°F, gas mark 6)

2 tablespoons olive oil
2 tablespoons water
1 large onion, peeled and chopped
1 large carrot, peeled and finely chopped

1 medium red pepper, de-seeded and finely chopped
Freshly ground black pepper
1oz (30g) wholemeal breadcrumbs
1 level teaspoon ground ginger
⅛ level teaspoon ground cloves
1½ lb (680g) rolled loin of pork, trimmed of fat
2 tablespoons lemon juice
7fl oz (200ml) vegetable or chicken
stock

The pork is trimmed of fat but, moistened from within by a savoury stuffing and from outside by stock, it cooks to tempting succulence.

1 Heat one tablespoon of the oil in a frying pan with the water and cook the onion, carrot and red pepper in it over a low heat for 6-8 minutes, until the vegetables are soft. Season with black pepper and stir in the breadcrumbs, ginger and cloves to make a well-blended stuffing.

2 Cut a pocket in the centre of the pork for the filling. Push in the stuffing, but not too tightly or it will be squeezed out as the meat shrinks during cooking. Sprinkle the lemon juice over the meat and rub it in well.

3 Heat the remaining oil in a small roasting tin over a moderately high direct heat and quickly brown the stuffed pork all over. Pour the stock in with the meat and bring it to the boil, then put the tin in the heated oven and cook the pork for 20 minutes. Lower the heat to 180°C (350°F, gas mark 4) and cook for another 20 minutes, basting from time to time with the stock, until the pork is cooked through.

4 Lift the pork onto a hot serving plate, cover it loosely with foil and leave it to rest for 10 minutes. Skim off and discard the fat from the juices in the roasting tin.

5 Reheat the roasting juices while you cut the meat into slices. Spoon the juices round the meat before serving.

New potatoes, mangetout and tiny sweetcorn cobs add bite and extra colour to the tender slices of pork.

> **TIP**
> *To make the pocket for the stuffing, push a very sharp long-bladed knife through the centre of the meat from end to end. Move the knife gently from side to side until the slit is large enough to hold the stuffing.*

Apple and cider, popular ingredients in the cooking of Normandy, mellow the lively herb flavouring in the sauce as well as the meatballs.

Normandy meatballs and cider sauce

ONE SERVING	
CALORIES	340
TOTAL FAT	14g
SATURATED FAT	5g
CARBOHYDRATES	21g
ADDED SUGAR	0
FIBRE	3g
SODIUM	295mg

SERVES 4
PREPARATION TIME: 15 minutes
COOKING TIME: 25 minutes
OVEN: Preheat to 200°C (400°F, gas mark 6)

1lb (450g) boneless pork with fat removed, minced
3oz (85g) wholemeal breadcrumbs
2oz (60g) ready-to-use stoned prunes,
finely chopped
1 dessert apple, about 4oz (115g), peeled, cored
and finely chopped
1oz (30g) walnuts, chopped
1 level tablespoon coarsely chopped fresh sage,
or 1 level teaspoon dried sage
⅛ level teaspoon salt
Freshly ground black pepper
1 egg, size 2, lightly beaten
½ oz (15g) slightly salted butter
1 small onion, peeled and finely chopped
1 level tablespoon plain flour
¼ pint (150ml) vegetable or chicken stock
¼ pint (150ml) medium sweet cider
1 level tablespoon chopped fresh parsley
2 level tablespoons low-fat natural yoghurt
Sage leaves to garnish

1 Mix the pork, breadcrumbs, prunes, apple, walnuts and sage, season with salt and pepper and work in the egg to bind the mixture. Divide it into 20 pieces and roll each into a ball.

2 Put the pork balls into a nonstick roasting tin and cook in the heated oven for about 25 minutes, or until golden brown.

3 Meanwhile, melt the butter in a saucepan, and cook the onion in it gently for about 5 minutes, or until soft. Stir in the flour and cook for 30 seconds. Gradually stir in the stock and cider and bring to the boil, stirring continuously. Mix in the parsley, season with pepper and set the sauce aside.

4 When the meatballs are cooked, stir the yoghurt into the sauce and reheat, but do not boil or it will curdle. Pour into a warmed jug for serving. Turn the meatballs into a serving dish and garnish with sage leaves.

Mashed potato goes well with the meatballs, while crisp spring greens or broccoli will make a pleasing contrast with their tenderness.

Pork with roasted peppers

SERVES 4
PREPARATION TIME: 30 minutes
COOKING TIME: 25 minutes

ONE SERVING	
CALORIES	300
TOTAL FAT	9g
SATURATED FAT	2g
CARBOHYDRATES	27g
ADDED SUGAR	0
FIBRE	4g
SODIUM	185mg

Roasting the sweet red peppers enhances their characteristically smoky flavour. Partnered by tomatoes and sharpened by a little vinegar and cayenne, they give a vivid touch of the hot south to the pork.

2 large red peppers
1lb (450g) boned shoulder of pork with fat removed, cut into 4 slices
1 level tablespoon plain flour
1 tablespoon olive oil
1 medium onion, peeled and chopped
2 cloves garlic, peeled and crushed
2lb (900g) tinned tomatoes, drained and chopped
2oz (60g) sultanas
1 tablespoon red wine vinegar
¼ level teaspoon cayenne pepper
1 level teaspoon dried oregano

1 Grill the peppers under a moderate heat for 10-12 minutes, turning often, until they are browned all over. Put them in a bowl, cover with a clean damp cloth and set aside. When they are cool enough to handle, pull off their skins, working over a bowl to catch any juice. Remove the seeds and cut the flesh into strips.

2 Meanwhile, put the pork slices between sheets of greaseproof paper and beat them with a rolling pin until they are very thin. Coat the slices lightly with the flour.

3 Heat the oil in a frying pan, and cook the pork slices in it over a moderate heat for 4 minutes on each side. Lay the slices on a plate covered with kitchen paper and set aside.

4 Fry the onion and garlic gently in the same pan for 5 minutes, until softened. Stir in the tomatoes, sultanas, vinegar, cayenne pepper, oregano and any juice from the grilled peppers. Bring to the boil, reduce the heat, cover and cook for 5 minutes, stirring occasionally.

5 Put the pork slices in the sauce, scatter in the pepper strips, cover and heat through for about 5 minutes.

Fresh pasta and a mixed green salad make simple accompaniments for the subtly flavoured pork and its sauce.

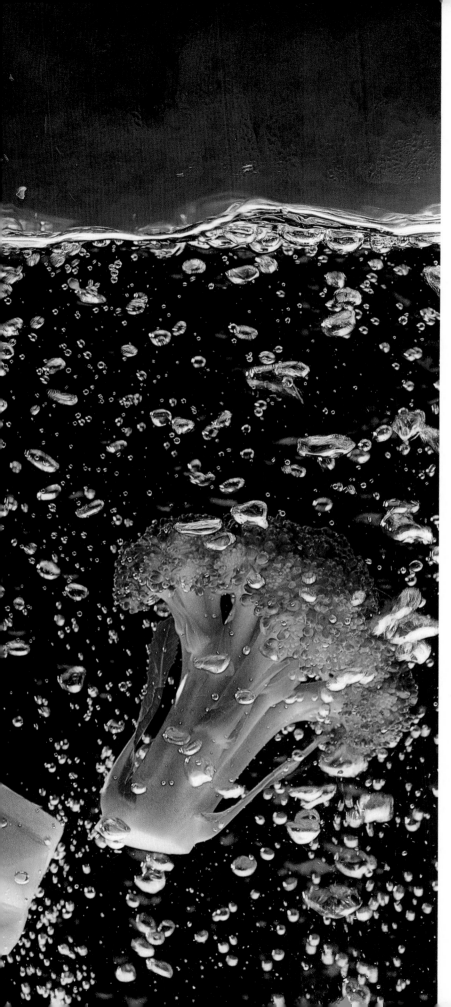

VEGETABLE
SIDE DISHES

Whether blanched or steamed for crispness, or baked or roasted to intensify the taste, vegetables are one of nature's most bountiful sources of nourishment, offering fibre, vital minerals and vitamins, and some protein as well. Here are ideas for presenting them — some in novel combinations, others using healthy ways of creating traditional rich flavours.

Broad beans in parsley sauce

SERVES 4
PREPARATION TIME: 20 minutes
COOKING TIME: 8 minutes

3lb (1.4kg) fresh broad beans in their pods, to
give 1lb (450g) shelled beans
Freshly ground black pepper
4 level tablespoons Greek yoghurt
2 level tablespoons chopped fresh parsley
1 level teaspoon paprika

1 Bring 1¾ pints (1 litre) of unsalted water to
the boil in a large saucepan and cook the beans
in it, covered, for 8 minutes, or until tender.

2 Drain the beans well, season with pepper
and stir in the yoghurt, parsley and paprika.
Turn into a warmed dish and serve.

When broad beans are out of season, you can
use 1lb (450g) of frozen broad beans.

Green beans with dill dressing

SERVES 4
PREPARATION TIME: 10 minutes
COOKING TIME: 6 minutes

1lb (450g) fine green beans, tops and tails removed
½ oz (15g) slightly salted butter
2 teaspoons lemon juice
Freshly ground mixed peppercorns
2 level tablespoons chopped fresh dill, or ½ level
teaspoon dried dill

1 Cook the beans in unsalted boiling water for
3-4 minutes, until almost tender. Turn into a
colander, rinse under a cold tap and drain.

2 Melt the butter in a large, nonstick frying
pan over a moderate heat until it sizzles. Cook
the beans in it, tossing and stirring, for
2-3 minutes. Season with the lemon juice and
pepper, mix in the dill and turn into a warmed
serving dish.

> **TIP**
> To top and tail
> beans quickly, hold
> a bunch loosely, tap
> down on a board to
> align the tips,
> then cut off the
> tips with scissors
> or a sharp knife.
> Tap to align the
> stem ends and cut
> them off.

Runner beans with cherry tomatoes

SERVES 4
PREPARATION TIME: 10 minutes
COOKING TIME: 7 minutes

1lb (450g) runner beans with tops, tails
and strings removed, thinly sliced
2 teaspoons olive oil
12oz (340g) cherry tomatoes
2 level tablespoons chopped fresh basil,
or 1 level teaspoon dried basil
1 tablespoon red wine vinegar
Shredded basil to garnish

1 Bring 1in (25mm) of unsalted water to the
boil in a saucepan and cook the beans in it,
covered, for 3-4 minutes, until softening but
still slightly firm. Keep 2 tablespoons of the
cooking water, drain off the remainder and set
the beans aside.

2 Heat the oil in a frying pan and fry
the tomatoes in it over a moderately high
heat, shaking the pan frequently, for about
2 minutes, until the skins begin to split.

3 Stir in the basil, beans, reserved cooking
water and vinegar. Heat through for 3 minutes,
uncovered, tossing occasionally. Turn into a
warmed dish and garnish with the basil.

*Three contrasting dishes show the versatility of beans:
broad beans in a satisfyingly creamy yoghurt and
parsley sauce, fine green beans flavoured with butter
and dill, and crisp runner beans paired with
jewel-bright and juicy cherry tomatoes.*

Beetroots with horseradish sauce

SERVES 4
PREPARATION TIME: 15 minutes
COOKING TIME: 1 hour 30 minutes

1lb (450g) beetroots, with skin undamaged, washed
4oz (115g) low-fat natural yoghurt
2 level tablespoons freshly grated horseradish
3 level tablespoons chopped fresh dill
Freshly ground black pepper

1 Cook the beetroots in a large, covered pan of unsalted boiling water for 1 hour 30 minutes, until tender when pierced with a knife tip. Drain, peel off the skin and dice the flesh.

2 Mix the yoghurt, horseradish and half the dill in a dish, and season with pepper. Turn the beetroot in the sauce and sprinkle with the remaining dill.

You can cook the beetroots a day in advance, cool, cover and keep in the refrigerator. Before serving, peel and dice the beetroots and heat through in the sauce without boiling.

Simple steamed broccoli is dressed up with a rich and exuberant basil sauce and scattered with crunchy nuts, while the fire of horseradish and tartness of yoghurt blend with the mild sweetness of beetroots to create a piquant pink sauce.

Broccoli with basil sauce

SERVES 4
PREPARATION TIME: 10 minutes
COOKING TIME: 8 minutes

1¼ lb (550g) broccoli, trimmed and divided into florets
10 basil leaves, stems trimmed off

1 clove garlic, peeled
1½ oz (45g) pine nuts or shelled walnuts
½ oz (15g) grated Parmesan cheese
4 tablespoons vegetable stock
1 teaspoon lemon juice
Freshly ground black pepper
Basil leaves to garnish

1 Steam the broccoli for 6-8 minutes, until cooked but still slightly firm.

2 Meanwhile, prepare the sauce. Blend the trimmed basil leaves, garlic, two-thirds of the nuts and the Parmesan with the stock and

lemon juice in a food processor for about 30 seconds, or until smooth.

3 Turn the broccoli into a warmed dish. Season with pepper, pour on the sauce and garnish with the basil and remaining nuts.

> **TIP**
> *To ensure that the broccoli stems cook as quickly as the flowers, peel the outer layer off them with a sharp knife before cooking.*

ONE SERVING	
CALORIES	100
TOTAL FAT	5g
SATURATED FAT	1g
CARBOHYDRATES	6g
ADDED SUGAR	0
FIBRE	4g
SODIUM	15mg

Broccoli with sweet pepper

SERVES 4
PREPARATION TIME: 15 minutes
COOKING TIME: 10 minutes

4 teaspoons olive oil
1 small onion, peeled and chopped
2 cloves garlic, peeled and crushed
1 tablespoon water
1¼ lb (550g) broccoli, trimmed and divided into florets
1 small red pepper, de-seeded and cut into thick strips
1 level teaspoon dried oregano, crumbled

1 Heat the oil in a heavy-based saucepan and put in the onion, garlic, water, broccoli, red pepper and oregano. Cook, stirring, over a moderately high heat for 2 minutes.

2 Reduce the heat and simmer, covered, for about 6 minutes more, stirring frequently, until the broccoli is tender but still crisp. Turn into a warmed dish and serve at once.

The bright, contrasting colours and crisp textures are preserved by part stir-frying, part steaming.

This is a fresh and appetising way to serve cabbage, which blends particularly well with the full, savoury taste of Cheddar. The cabbage remains crunchy but soaks up the stock, which is enriched by wine.

Baked cabbage wedges with cheese

ONE SERVING	
CALORIES 80	
TOTAL FAT 5g	
SATURATED FAT 3g	
CARBOHYDRATES 3g	
ADDED SUGAR 0	
FIBRE 2g	
SODIUM 85mg	

SERVES 6
PREPARATION TIME: 20 minutes
COOKING TIME: 45 minutes
OVEN: Preheat to 200°C (400°F, gas mark 6)

1 savoy or other firm green cabbage, about 1½ lb (680g), trimmed, cored and cut into 6 wedges
6fl oz (175ml) chicken stock
4 tablespoons dry white wine
Freshly ground black pepper
½ oz (15g) slightly salted butter
3 level tablespoons white or wholemeal breadcrumbs
1½ oz (45g) grated mature Cheddar cheese
2 level tablespoons chopped fresh parsley

1 Arrange the cabbage wedges in a single layer in a shallow, flameproof casserole. Pour in the stock and wine, and season with pepper. Bring to the boil over a direct heat, then put the casserole in the heated oven, and cook for about 40 minutes, or until the cabbage is cooked but still crisp.

2 Meanwhile, melt the butter in a small, heavy-based saucepan and cook the breadcrumbs in it over a moderate heat for about 2 minutes, stirring, until they are lightly browned. Remove from the heat and set aside.

3 When the cabbage is cooked, sprinkle the breadcrumbs and the Cheddar over the top and put the casserole under a hot grill for 2-3 minutes, or until the cheese is golden brown. Sprinkle with the parsley before serving.

Jerusalem artichokes braised in wine

SERVES 4
PREPARATION TIME: 15 minutes
COOKING TIME: 45 minutes

1 tablespoon olive oil
2 cloves garlic, peeled and finely chopped
1 small onion, peeled and chopped
1½ lb (680g) Jerusalem artichokes, peeled and sliced
4fl oz (115ml) dry white wine
4fl oz (115ml) vegetable stock
1 fresh bouquet garni
½ level teaspoon freshly grated nutmeg
Freshly ground black pepper
1 level tablespoon chopped fresh parsley
Sprigs of fresh herbs to garnish

1 Heat the oil in a large frying pan and cook the garlic and onion in it gently for 5 minutes.

2 Stir in the Jerusalem artichokes and cook for 5 minutes, turning the slices over several times to colour lightly. Pour on the wine and stock and put in the bouquet garni. Bring to the boil, then reduce the heat, partially cover the pan and simmer for about 35 minutes, or until the artichokes are tender and most of the liquid has evaporated. Stir gently from time to time to make sure that the artichokes are not sticking at the bottom of the pan.

3 Remove the bouquet garni, sprinkle in the nutmeg and season with pepper. Turn the artichokes into a warmed serving dish and scatter the parsley over them. Garnish with the herb sprigs before serving.

If you cannot find herbs for a fresh bouquet garni, you can use a made-up sachet.

TIP
To prevent the artichoke slices from going brown, drop them as fast as you cut them into a large bowl of cold water with a few drops of lemon juice added. Blot the slices quickly with kitchen paper just before they go in the pan.

A light seasoning of nutmeg and pepper highlights the delicate flavour absorbed by the artichokes during gentle braising in white wine, herbs and stock.

Even a small amount of flavoured olive oil can penetrate the flesh of a straightforward baked potato and transform it into a golden treat.

Baked garlic potatoes

ONE SERVING	
CALORIES 140	
TOTAL FAT 1g	
SATURATED FAT 0	
CARBOHYDRATES 30g	
ADDED SUGAR 0	
FIBRE 3g	
SODIUM 75mg	

SERVES 4
PREPARATION TIME: 5 minutes
COOKING TIME: 1 hour
OVEN: Preheat to 220°C (425°F, gas mark 7)

2 large baking potatoes, well scrubbed
1 teaspoon olive oil
⅛ level teaspoon salt
1 clove garlic, peeled and crushed
¼ level teaspoon paprika

1 Cut the potatoes in half lengthways and use a small sharp knife to score the cut surface deeply with a crisscross pattern. Arrange the potatoes on a baking sheet.

2 Mix the oil, salt and garlic, and brush the scored surfaces with the mixture. Sprinkle the paprika evenly over them, then bake in the heated oven for 1 hour, or until the potatoes are tender and their tops golden brown.

For a more strongly spiced flavour, add ¼ level teaspoon each of ground cumin, ground coriander and cayenne pepper to the oil mixture before brushing it on the potatoes.

Curried potatoes

ONE SERVING

CALORIES 150

TOTAL FAT 4g

SATURATED FAT 1g

CARBOHYDRATES 28g

ADDED SUGAR 0

FIBRE 3g

SODIUM 15mg

Traditional Indian herbs and spices are combined with stock to create a curry coating for the potato slices. This dish is delicious with cold meats.

SERVES 4
PREPARATION TIME: *15 minutes*
COOKING TIME: *30 minutes*

1 tablespoon olive oil
½ level teaspoon fennel seeds
1 level teaspoon cumin seeds
1 clove garlic, peeled and crushed
2 level teaspoons peeled and grated root ginger
2 level teaspoons ground cumin
2 level teaspoons ground coriander
½ level teaspoon ground turmeric
¼ level teaspoon cayenne pepper
1 level teaspoon paprika
1½ lb (680g) small potatoes, peeled and cut into thick slices
¾ pint (425ml) vegetable or chicken stock
2 level tablespoons chopped fresh coriander or parsley

1 Heat the oil in a large frying pan and stir the fennel and cumin seeds, garlic and ginger in it over a high heat for 30 seconds. Stir in the ground cumin, coriander, turmeric, cayenne and paprika and cook for a further 30 seconds.

2 Add the potato slices and stir until they are evenly coated with the spice mixture. Pour in the stock and bring to the boil, then lower the heat, cover and simmer for about 30 minutes, occasionally stirring gently, until the potatoes are tender and most of the stock has been absorbed, leaving just a coating of sauce.

3 Sprinkle the potatoes with the chopped coriander or parsley before serving.

You can use ready-mixed curry powder instead of ground cumin, coriander and turmeric.

New potatoes with creamy mint sauce

SERVES 4
PREPARATION TIME: 10 minutes
COOKING TIME: 15 minutes

1½ lb (680g) small new potatoes with skins on,
well washed
10 fresh mint leaves
1 level tablespoon snipped fresh chives
6oz (175g) Greek yoghurt
¼ level teaspoon cayenne pepper or freshly
ground black pepper
¼ level teaspoon paprika
Chives or mint sprigs to garnish

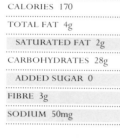

ONE SERVING

CALORIES 170

TOTAL FAT 4g

SATURATED FAT 2g

CARBOHYDRATES 28g

ADDED SUGAR 0

FIBRE 3g

SODIUM 50mg

1 Steam the potatoes for about 15 minutes,
or until they are just tender.

2 Meanwhile, put the mint leaves in boiling
water for 10 seconds, then drain and
immediately plunge them into cold water.
Pat the leaves dry with kitchen paper and
roughly snip them with scissors. Mix the mint
and snipped chives into the yoghurt, and
season with the cayenne or black pepper.

3 As soon as the potatoes are cooked, turn
them into a warmed serving dish, spoon the
sauce on them and dust with paprika. Garnish
with the chives or mint sprigs before serving.

*Minted new potatoes, a symbol of summer days, are
made even more tempting by adding creamy yoghurt.*

Sesame potatoes

SERVES 4
PREPARATION TIME: 10 minutes
COOKING TIME: 1 hour
OVEN: Preheat to 200°C (400°F, gas mark 6)

1½ lb (680g) equal-sized potatoes, peeled
1 tablespoon sesame oil
2 level tablespoons sesame seeds

1 Make vertical parallel cuts in each potato, about ¼ inch (6mm) apart and almost down to the base. Pat the potatoes with kitchen paper to dry them well.

2 Brush the potatoes sparingly with the oil and press the top of each firmly into the sesame seeds.

3 Put the potatoes in a lightly oiled baking tin, coated side up. Bake in the heated oven for about 1 hour, or until they are tender inside and crisply browned outside.

ONE SERVING	
CALORIES	165
TOTAL FAT	6g
SATURATED FAT	1g
CARBOHYDRATES	25g
ADDED SUGAR	0
FIBRE	2g
SODIUM	10mg

You can give potatoes the full and satisfying taste of orthodox roast potatoes, but use only a tiny amount of oil, or none at all. The puffy slices and the crunchy sesame-coated potatoes are perfect partners for a Sunday roast.

Potato slices

ONE SERVING	
CALORIES	110
TOTAL FAT	0
SATURATED FAT	0
CARBOHYDRATES	25g
ADDED SUGAR	0
FIBRE	2g
SODIUM	10mg

SERVES 4
PREPARATION TIME: 10 minutes
COOKING TIME: 40 minutes
OVEN: Preheat to 220°C (425°F, gas mark 7)

1½ lb (680g) baking potatoes, peeled and washed

1 Cut the potatoes into ½ in (13mm) slices with a crinkle potato cutter or a sharp knife. Dry the slices thoroughly on both sides with kitchen paper.

2 Spread the potato slices out in a single layer on a nonstick baking tray and bake in the heated oven for 20 minutes. Turn the potatoes over and cook for about 20 minutes more, or until golden brown, tender in the centre and slightly puffed.

Spinach and rice cakes

ONE SERVING

CALORIES 245

TOTAL FAT 5g

SATURATED FAT 2g

CARBOHYDRATES 46g

ADDED SUGAR 0

FIBRE 3g

SODIUM 150mg

Sweet-tasting water chestnuts give these upturned speckled cups of astringent spinach and plump rice a slight crunch and a touch of the exotic.

SERVES 4
PREPARATION TIME: *10 minutes*
COOKING TIME: *20 minutes*

7oz (200g) long grain rice
1lb (450g) fresh spinach, trimmed and washed
½oz (15g) slightly salted butter
2oz (60g) water chestnuts, finely chopped
2 tablespoons lemon juice
Freshly ground black pepper

1   Cook the rice.

2   Meanwhile, put the spinach in a saucepan without water. Cover and cook over a low heat for about 5 minutes, until softened.

3   Pour the spinach into a colander, press out as much liquid as possible with a wooden spoon, then chop the spinach finely. Melt the butter in the same saucepan and reheat the cooked spinach in the butter over a gentle heat for 1-2 minutes, stirring continuously.

4   Mix the spinach with the rice, water chestnuts and lemon juice, and season with pepper. Divide the mixture between four lightly oiled dariole moulds and press it down, or press all the mixture into an oiled shallow dish. Leave to stand for 1 minute, then turn out upside-down onto a warmed serving dish.

You can use 10oz (275g) of frozen leaf spinach instead of fresh spinach. Cook it gently without any water until it is completely thawed, and break it up in the pan with a wooden spoon before turning it into a sieve or colander to press out the liquid.

The sharpness of the apples makes a mouthwatering contrast to the sweetness of the potatoes in this stylish, unusual dish which is an ideal accompaniment to serve with pork.

TIP
Use Cox-type or Granny Smith apples. Their strong, sharp flavour and crisp flesh give the best taste and texture in this dish.

ONE SERVING	
CALORIES	130
TOTAL FAT	3g
SATURATED FAT	1g
CARBOHYDRATES	26g
ADDED SUGAR	0
FIBRE	3g
SODIUM	70mg

Sweet potatoes with apples

SERVES 4
PREPARATION TIME: 10 minutes
COOKING TIME: 40 minutes
OVEN: Preheat to 190°C (375°F, gas mark 5)

½ oz (15g) polyunsaturated margarine
1lb (450g) sweet potatoes, peeled and cut diagonally into thin slices
8oz (225g) dessert apples, peeled, cored and thinly sliced into rings
¼ level teaspoon freshly grated nutmeg

1 Grease a shallow, ovenproof dish with a little of the margarine. Arrange half the potatoes overlapping in the dish and cover with the apple rings. Arrange the remaining potato slices on top, dot with the remaining margarine and sprinkle with the nutmeg.

2 Cover and bake in the heated oven for 30 minutes. Uncover and bake for 10 minutes more, or until the potatoes are tender and golden brown on top.

DESSERTS

Ices and gâteaux, puddings and pies end a meal with a touch of luxury. When the fat and sugar have been carefully controlled, a moderate portion does no harm in a generally healthy diet. This selection of desserts makes the most of fresh fruits in season for the fibre they contribute.

Almond and raspberry meringue

SERVES 8
PREPARATION TIME: 30 minutes,
plus 1 hour to cool
COOKING TIME: 1 hour 30 minutes–2 hours
OVEN: Preheat to 140°C (275°F, gas mark 1)

1½ oz (45g) blanched almonds, finely chopped
and lightly toasted
3½ oz (100g) caster sugar
1 level tablespoon cornflour
4 egg whites, size 2
⅛ level teaspoon cream of tartar
12oz (340g) fresh raspberries, or frozen
raspberries, thawed
5oz (150g) Greek yoghurt

ONE SERVING

CALORIES 125

TOTAL FAT 5g

SATURATED FAT 1g

CARBOHYDRATES 17g

ADDED SUGAR 13g

FIBRE 1g

SODIUM 50mg

TIP
As a guide for spreading out the meringue mixture, pencil a circle firmly on each of the squares of baking paper, drawing it round an upturned plate. Turn the paper over so that the circle is on the underside but still visible.

1 Line two baking sheets with 12in (30cm) squares of nonstick baking paper.

2 Reserve a quarter of the almonds. Mix the rest with 1 tablespoon of the sugar and the cornflour. Whisk the egg whites until frothy. Add the cream of tartar and 1 tablespoon of sugar and whisk until the mixture forms soft peaks. Keep whisking, adding 1 tablespoon of sugar at a time, until the meringue is stiff and shiny. Whisk in the cornflour mixture.

3 Divide the meringue between the two lined baking sheets and spread with a palette knife into rounds 9½ in (24cm) in diameter. Mark swirls on the top of the meringues. Sprinkle the reserved almonds over one meringue.

4 Bake the meringues in the heated oven for 1½–2 hours, or until dry but slightly soft in the centre so that they give when gently pressed. Leave to cool on the baking sheets for 1 hour.

5 Press 4oz (115g) of the raspberries through a nylon sieve to make a purée.

6 Peel the baking paper off the meringues. Place the meringue without nuts flat-side up on a serving plate and spread the yoghurt on it. Arrange all but 2 tablespoons of the fruit over the yoghurt, and trickle the purée over it. Place the second meringue on top, nut side up, and decorate with the remaining raspberries. Refrigerate until serving time.

You can use hulled loganberries or strawberries in place of the raspberries.

A slightly tart filling of thick yoghurt and whole and puréed raspberries is sandwiched between meringues lightly flavoured with almonds.

Black Forest gâteau

SERVES 12
PREPARATION TIME: 40 minutes,
plus 1 hour to cool
COOKING TIME: 20 minutes
OVEN: Preheat to 180°C (350°F, gas mark 4)

ONE SERVING	
CALORIES 175	
TOTAL FAT 6g	
SATURATED FAT 3g	
CARBOHYDRATES 27g	
ADDED SUGAR 16g	
FIBRE 1g	
SODIUM 95mg	

1oz (30g) cocoa
2oz (60g) plain flour
6oz (175g) caster sugar
8 egg whites, size 2
1 level teaspoon cream of tartar
1½ teaspoons vanilla extract
2 tablespoons cold water
1 level teaspoon gelatine
2 level teaspoons soft dark brown sugar
1 level tablespoon cornflour
Finely grated rind of ½ lemon and 1 teaspoon juice
15oz (425g) tinned stoned black cherries in unsweetened juice, drained and juice reserved
4fl oz (115ml) double cream
4fl oz (115ml) evaporated milk, well chilled
Fresh cherries for decoration

1 Line the bases of two nonstick sponge cake tins, 8½ in (21cm) in diameter, with nonstick baking paper. Sift the cocoa, flour and 5oz (150g) of the caster sugar into a large bowl.

2 Beat the egg whites with an electric or rotary hand whisk until they will hold soft peaks. While whisking, add the cream of tartar, the remaining caster sugar and 1 teaspoon of the vanilla extract.

3 Fold the cocoa mixture gently into the egg whites, a third at a time, using a spatula. Divide the mixture between the two sponge cake tins and spread evenly.

4 Bake the sponges in the heated oven for about 20 minutes, or until they are risen and springy to the touch when lightly pressed at the centre. Leave to cool, then run a spatula round the edge of each sponge and turn out onto a wire rack. Remove the baking paper.

5 Pour the water into a small basin, sprinkle the gelatine evenly over the water and leave for 5 minutes for the gelatine to swell.

6 Blend the brown sugar, cornflour and lemon rind in a saucepan with the reserved juice from the cherries. Bring to the boil, stirring continuously. Reduce the heat and simmer for 1 minute, still stirring, until the sauce becomes thick and clear. Remove from the heat.

7 Check the cherries to make sure there are no stones in them, then stir into the sauce and leave to cool.

8 Stand the bowl of gelatine in a saucepan of hot water until the gelatine dissolves. Leave to cool. Whisk the cream and remaining vanilla extract until the cream forms soft peaks. Whisk the evaporated milk and lemon juice until the mixture becomes very thick, then whisk in the cooled gelatine. Gently fold in the whipped cream.

9 Put one sponge onto a serving plate, top side down. Spread with the cherry filling and then cover with half the whipped cream. Place the other sponge on it, top side up. Pipe rosettes of the remaining cream on top of the cake and decorate with fresh cherries. Refrigerate until 30 minutes before serving time.

TIP
For a delicate vanilla flavour, use vanilla sugar instead of caster sugar and vanilla extract. Keep a vanilla pod in a storage jar of caster sugar to flavour it. Top up the jar each time you use some of the sugar.

In this skilful adaptation of the originally indulgent German gâteau, the fragrant, juicy cherry filling and thick whipped cream are still sandwiched between feather-light cakes of chocolate sponge to make a special-occasion dessert. But the usually high calorie and fat content has been significantly reduced by leaving out the egg yolks and whisking up a delicate, creamy vanilla mousse for the filling and topping.

Crème brûlée

SERVES 4
PREPARATION TIME: 15 minutes,
plus 2 hours to cool and chill
COOKING TIME: 20 minutes

3 egg yolks, size 2
½ oz (15g) cornflour
½ oz (15g) caster sugar
14fl oz (400ml) skimmed milk
2 level tablespoons Greek yoghurt
1 teaspoon vanilla extract
1 small banana
6oz (175g) fresh raspberries
1oz (30g) demerara sugar

ONE SERVING

CALORIES 180

TOTAL FAT 6g

SATURATED FAT 2g

CARBOHYDRATES 27g

ADDED SUGAR 12g

FIBRE 1g

SODIUM 70mg

1 Whisk the egg yolks, cornflour and caster sugar in a bowl.

2 Heat the milk until it is hot but not boiling, and whisk it into the egg yolk mixture. Place the bowl over a saucepan of gently simmering water and stir continuously with a wooden spoon for about 20 minutes, or until the custard has thickened sufficiently to coat the back of the spoon.

3 Remove the bowl of custard from the saucepan and stir in the yoghurt and vanilla.

4 Peel and slice the banana and mix it with the raspberries. Divide the fruit between four ¼ pint (150ml) ramekin dishes. Pour a share of the custard into each dish, leave to cool, then put in the refrigerator for about 1½ hours, until very cold.

5 Sprinkle the demerara sugar evenly over the top of the four dishes, leave to stand for 5 minutes, then put under a hot grill for only about 20 seconds to melt and brown the sugar. Serve immediately, or return to the refrigerator to keep chilled until serving time.

Raspberries and banana nestle under the crème brûlée, 'burnt cream', in this reduced-fat adaptation of a rich pudding. As in the traditional version, the smooth vanilla custard is topped by a crackly, toffee-flavoured crust.

Fruit salad

ONE SERVING

CALORIES 160

TOTAL FAT 0

SATURATED FAT 0

CARBOHYDRATES 38g

ADDED SUGAR 0

FIBRE 4g

SODIUM 45mg

SERVES 4
PREPARATION TIME: 20 minutes,
plus 1-2 hours to refrigerate

1 medium, ripe melon, about 1½ lb (680g)
2 medium oranges with peel and pith
pared off, segments cut from membranes
and any pips removed

8oz (225g) strawberries, hulled and sliced
6oz (175g) seedless green grapes, peeled
and halved
1½ level teaspoons finely grated orange rind
4fl oz (115ml) freshly squeezed and strained
orange juice
2 medium bananas
Fresh mint sprigs for decoration

A medley of colourful fresh fruits, full of natural sweetness and refreshed with real orange juice, makes an enjoyably light end to a meal.

TIP
*Do not peel and
slice the bananas
until there is plenty
of juice in the salad
to coat them. The
flesh quickly goes
brown when exposed
to air.*

1 Halve and de-seed the melon, take out the
flesh with a melon scoop and put the balls into
a large bowl. Mix in the orange segments.

2 Stir the strawberries, grapes and orange rind
into the salad and pour on the orange juice.

3 Peel and slice the bananas and mix them
gently into the salad. Cover and refrigerate for
1-2 hours, until 30 minutes before serving.

4 Just before serving, spoon the salad into a
serving bowl and decorate it with the mint.

You may prefer to serve the fruit salad in
individual serving bowls and top each with a
sprig of mint. For a sweeter fruit salad, you can
add 1 level tablespoon of golden sultanas. For a
special occasion you can hand round a small
bowl of Greek yoghurt for each diner to have
a spoonful with the salad.

Mango choux ring

ONE SERVING

CALORIES 265

TOTAL FAT 13g

SATURATED FAT 3g

CARBOHYDRATES 33g

ADDED SUGAR 8g

FIBRE 2g

SODIUM 125mg

TIP
To ensure that the choux pastry is light and crisp, add only about 2 teaspoons of egg to the paste at a time and beat vigorously before adding any more.

SERVES 6
PREPARATION TIME: 40 minutes, plus 1-2 hours to refrigerate
COOKING TIME: 40 minutes
OVEN: Preheat to 220°C (425°F, gas mark 7)

For the filling:
1½ oz (45g) cornflour
1½ oz (45g) caster sugar
¾ pint (425ml) semi-skimmed milk
2 tablespoons rum, or 1 teaspoon vanilla extract
1½ oz (45g) blanched almonds
6 level tablespoons Greek yoghurt
1 large ripe mango, peeled, stoned and thinly sliced

For the choux pastry:
¼ pint (150ml) water
2oz (60g) polyunsaturated margarine
2½ oz (70g) plain flour
1 egg, plus 1 egg white, size 2

1 Blend the cornflour and ½ oz (15g) of the sugar with the milk in a saucepan, and slowly bring to the boil, stirring continuously. Cook for 2-3 minutes, still stirring all the time.

2 Remove from the heat and beat in the rum or vanilla extract. Pour the custard into a bowl and put a disc of wetted nonstick baking paper directly on the custard to cover it completely. Leave to cool, then refrigerate for 1-2 hours.

3 Pencil a circle 7in (18cm) in diameter firmly on a sheet of nonstick baking paper, using an upturned plate as a guide. Turn the paper over and lay it on a baking sheet.

4 To prepare the choux pastry ring, slowly heat the water and the margarine in a saucepan, until the margarine has melted. Bring to the boil, tip in all the flour and quickly stir it in. Beat over the heat until the mixture forms a ball of stiff paste. Remove from the heat and cool for 3-4 minutes.

5 Whisk the whole egg and the egg white and beat little by little into the cooled paste, using a hand-held electric mixer or a wooden spoon. Beat well between each addition of egg.

6 Put spoonfuls of the choux paste barely touching one another in a ring on the baking sheet, placing them just inside the pencilled circle. Alternatively, pipe the choux paste through a large, plain nozzle to form a thick ring just inside the pencilled circle.

7 Bake in the heated oven for 30 minutes until well risen, golden brown and firm to the touch. Remove from the oven and pierce with a knife in several places round the side of the ring, to let out the steam. Put the ring back in the oven for a further 10 minutes.

8 Lift the choux ring onto a wire rack and cut in half horizontally. Carefully separate the two halves and scoop out and discard any uncooked pastry from the centre. Leave the ring halves to cool completely.

9 Put the remaining caster sugar and the almonds in a small saucepan, set over a very low heat and stir until the sugar dissolves and turns to a golden brown caramel; watch all the time, as it quickly burns and goes bitter. Pour onto a plate lined with nonstick baking paper, and leave to cool. When cold, grind finely in a food processor, or put between sheets of nonstick paper and crush firmly with a rolling pin on a sturdy surface to make a praline.

10 Remove the chilled custard from the refrigerator and whisk until smooth. Whisk in the yoghurt and all but two teaspoons of the praline mixture.

11 Just before serving time, put the bottom half of the choux ring on a flat serving plate and fill with the custard. Arrange the mango slices on top, then cover with the top half of the choux ring. Sprinkle on the remaining praline.

Puffs of airy choux pastry, sprinkled with a golden almond praline, form a ring filled with a creamy, rum-flavoured custard and slices of mellow mango. An intriguing acid-sweet flavour and silky texture make this tropical fruit an ideal, although unusual, partner for such a crisp, light pastry. You can put a few pansies, primroses or nasturtiums in the centre for a particularly festive presentation.

Peach and almond strudel

SERVES 6
PREPARATION TIME: 30 minutes
COOKING TIME: 45 minutes
OVEN: Preheat to 200°C (400°F, gas mark 6)

$1\frac{1}{2}$ oz (45g) ground almonds
1 level tablespoon caster sugar
1 level teaspoon ground mixed spice
Finely grated rind of 1 lemon
$1\frac{1}{2}$ oz (45g) wholemeal breadcrumbs
6oz (175g) filo pastry sheets
1oz (30g) polyunsaturated margarine, melted
4 large ripe peaches, skinned, stoned and sliced

1   Mix the almonds, sugar, spice and lemon rind with 1oz (30g) of the breadcrumbs.

2   On a large clean teacloth, lay half the sheets of pastry, trimmed as necessary and with edges overlapping, to form a rectangle about 20×16in (51×40cm). Arrange the rectangle so that one of its long sides is nearest to you. Brush lightly with melted margarine. Arrange a second layer of pastry sheets on top in the same way and brush with a little more margarine.

3   Spread the ground almond mixture in a 4in (10cm) strip along the side nearest to you, setting it in 2in (50mm) from the edge. Arrange the peach slices on top of the mixture.

4   Fold the two short sides in by 1in (25mm), and fold the clear 2in (50mm) strip of pastry over the peaches. Lift the edge of the teacloth nearest to you so that the strudel begins to roll away from you. Keep lifting until the strudel is completely rolled. Carefully lay the strudel, seam side down, on a nonstick baking sheet.

5   Brush the remaining margarine over the strudel and sprinkle with the remaining breadcrumbs. Bake in the heated oven for about 45 minutes, or until the pastry is golden brown and crisp. Serve the strudel warm.

When fresh peaches are unavailable use $1\frac{3}{4}$ lb (800g) of unsweetened tinned peach halves, drained, dried with kitchen paper and sliced. For a special occasion, sift 1 level teaspoon of icing sugar over the strudel and put a teaspoon of Greek yoghurt beside each serving.

....
ONE SERVING
CALORIES 215
....
TOTAL FAT 9g
....
SATURATED FAT 1g
....
CARBOHYDRATES 29g
....
ADDED SUGAR 3g
....
FIBRE 3g
....
SODIUM 180mg
....

TIP
*If the peach skins
will not pull off
easily, put the fruit
in a heatproof bowl,
pour boiling water
over them, leave for
1 minute then rinse
with cold water.
The skin will come
away easily.*

Melting, spiced almond paste and fresh peach slices in a wafer-thin wrapping create this tempting variation of the Viennese apple strudel.

Peach sorbet

SERVES 4
*PREPARATION TIME: 20 minutes, plus 5 hours
to chill and freeze*

3½ oz (100g) granulated sugar
7fl oz (200ml) water
*4 large ripe peaches, skinned, halved and stoned,
and sliced*
2 tablespoons lemon or lime juice
1 small ripe peach, sliced, for decoration

1 Put the sugar and water in a saucepan and
stir over a low heat until the sugar dissolves,
then bring to the boil and boil for 1 minute.
Take the syrup off the heat and let it cool for
30 minutes. Pour it into a bowl, cover and
refrigerate for 1½ hours.

2 Blend the peach slices in a food processor
for 1 minute, then add the syrup and the lemon
or lime juice, and blend for 30 seconds more.
Pour the mixture into a plastic box, cover and
freeze for about 3 hours or until hard.

3 Peel and slice the small peach. Cut the
frozen peach mixture into large pieces and
blend in a food processor for 10 seconds, until
soft. Spoon the sorbet into individual dishes
and decorate each serving with some peach
slices. Serve at once.

*The luscious crushed flesh of ripe peaches, mingled
with a syrup and enlivened with citrus juice, makes a
tingling-fresh, ice-cold pudding for summer days.*

ONE SERVING	
CALORIES	145
TOTAL FAT	0
SATURATED FAT	0
CARBOHYDRATES	37g
ADDED SUGAR	26g
FIBRE	2g
SODIUM	0

Plum cobbler

ONE SERVING	
CALORIES	280
TOTAL FAT	8g
SATURATED FAT	1g
CARBOHYDRATES	48g
ADDED SUGAR	8g
FIBRE	4g
SODIUM	245mg

SERVES 6
PREPARATION TIME: 30 minutes
COOKING TIME: 45 minutes
OVEN: Preheat to 200°C (400°F, gas mark 6)

1½ lb (680g) ripe Victoria plums or Spanish dessert plums, halved and stoned
1½ oz (45g) soft light brown sugar
1oz (30g) ground almonds
6 tablespoons water

For the topping:
6oz (175g) self-raising flour
2oz (60g) plain wholemeal flour
1 level teaspoon baking powder
1oz (30g) polyunsaturated margarine
1 egg, size 2, lightly beaten
7 tablespoons skimmed milk
1 teaspoon caster sugar

Mellow dessert plums, their juice thickened by ground almonds, are baked beneath thick rounds of low-fat scone pastry in this warming family pudding for autumn days.

1 Mix the plums with the brown sugar, ground almonds and water. Spread the mixture in an ovenproof dish 8in (20cm) in diameter.

2 To make the topping, combine the flours and baking powder in a bowl, and rub in the margarine. Pour in the egg and 6 tablespoons of the milk, and mix to form a soft dough. Knead to an even texture on a lightly floured surface.

3 Roll out the dough on a lightly floured surface to ½ in (13mm) thick. Use a fluted 2½ in (65mm) cutter to cut rounds from the dough. Knead and roll the trimmings and cut out more rounds to make 12 in all. Lay them,

slightly overlapping, in a circle round the dish and brush with the remaining milk.

4 Bake in the heated oven for 45 minutes, or until the rounds are golden and the plums soft. Cover with greaseproof paper after 30 minutes so the top does not brown too much. Sprinkle the cobbler with the caster sugar and serve hot.

If you like, you can add 1 teaspoon of vanilla extract to the dough. A spoonful of Greek yoghurt on each serving would add a touch of luxury. If you cannot get ripe Victoria or Spanish dessert plums you can use a cooking variety, but you might have to add more sugar.

Strawberry charlotte

SERVES 8
PREPARATION TIME: 50 minutes, plus 3 hours
to refrigerate
COOKING TIME: 10 minutes
OVEN: Preheat to 220°C (425°F, gas mark 7)

3 eggs, size 2
4oz (115g) caster sugar
3oz (85g) plain flour
1½ lb (680g) strawberries, hulled, washed
and dried
7oz (200g) Greek yoghurt
7oz (200g) low-fat natural yoghurt
6 tablespoons cold water
1oz (30g) powdered gelatine
Sprigs of mint and whole strawberries for decoration

1 Line a swiss-roll tin, 15×12in (38×30cm),
with nonstick baking paper.

2 Whisk the eggs and half the sugar in a bowl
with an electric or rotary hand whisk until
fluffy and so thick that a ribbon of mixture
trailed on it from the whisk stays on the
surface. Sift the flour over the mixture and fold
it in gently with a large metal spoon. Pour into
the swiss-roll tin and spread evenly. Bake in the
heated oven for about 8 minutes, or until well
risen, very lightly coloured and springy to
the touch. Turn onto a wire rack, remove the
baking paper and leave to cool.

3 Meanwhile blend two-thirds of the hulled
strawberries with the yoghurts and the rest of
the sugar in a food processor until smooth, and
pour into a bowl. Roughly chop the remaining
third of the strawberries and fold into the
strawberry and yoghurt mixture.

4 Pour the water into a small saucepan and
sprinkle the gelatine evenly over the surface.
Leave to stand for 5 minutes until the gelatine
swells and becomes opaque, then stir over a
low heat until dissolved. Quickly stir the hot
gelatine into the strawberry and yoghurt

ONE SERVING	
CALORIES	205
TOTAL FAT	5g
SATURATED FAT	2g
CARBOHYDRATES	30g
ADDED SUGAR	15g
FIBRE	1g
SODIUM	75mg

TIP
*Be sure to pat
the strawberries
thoroughly dry with
kitchen paper before
blending with the
yoghurts. If the
mixture is too
watery, the gelatine
will not set it.*

*This low-fat variation of a special-occasion dessert
has crushed fresh strawberries whisked to a pink
cream with thick yoghurt and encased in a delicate
sponge. Gelatine firms up the filling, holding it in
shape without affecting its refreshing lightness.*

mixture, then refrigerate the mixture for 5-10 minutes, until it is thickened but not set.

5 Meanwhile, cut across the sponge cake to make four strips and trim them to fit the bottom, sides and ends of a nonstick loaf tin 10×4½ in (25×12cm). Arrange the sponge with the unbrowned sides against the tin. Spoon in the strawberry and yoghurt mixture

and spread evenly. Cover the charlotte and put it in the refrigerator for 3 hours, or overnight, until the filling is firmly set.

6 If necessary, trim the sponge so that it is level with the top of the strawberry filling. Turn the charlotte onto a flat serving plate and decorate with sprigs of fresh mint and strawberries cut into thin slices.

Gooseberry pancakes

ONE SERVING	
CALORIES	245
TOTAL FAT	5g
SATURATED FAT	2g
CARBOHYDRATES	43g
ADDED SUGAR	11g
FIBRE	4g
SODIUM	65mg

SERVES 4
PREPARATION TIME: 20 minutes
COOKING TIME: 35 minutes
OVEN: Preheat to 190°C (375°F, gas mark 5)

Finely grated rind and juice of ½ orange
1oz (30g) soft light brown sugar
1lb (450g) ripe dessert gooseberries, topped and tailed
4oz (115g) plain wholemeal flour

1 egg, size 2, beaten
½ pint (285ml) semi-skimmed milk
2 teaspoons corn oil
Squares of greaseproof paper for stacking
1 level tablespoon demerara sugar

1 Gently heat the orange rind and juice with the light brown sugar in a saucepan, stirring to dissolve the sugar. Put in the gooseberries and simmer for about 10 minutes, stirring occasionally, until they are soft and the juice is slightly thickened. Leave to cool.

2 Put the flour in a mixing bowl, make a well in the centre and pour in the egg and half the milk. Stir well with a wooden spoon until the ingredients are combined, then beat until smooth. Stir in the remaining milk and pour the batter into a measuring jug.

3 Smear a little oil over the base of a nonstick frying pan 6in (15cm) in diameter. Heat it over a moderate heat until it gives off a slight haze. Pour one-eighth of the batter into the pan and quickly tilt the pan until the base is coated thinly. Cook until the top of the batter is set and the underside golden brown. Turn or toss the pancake over and cook the other side. Slide out onto a plate. Make seven more pancakes in the same way and put greaseproof paper between them as you stack them on the plate.

4 Lay the pancakes with the side cooked first down on the work surface. Divide the filling between the pancakes and spread evenly. Fold each one in half, then in half again to make a fan shape and overlap the fans in an ovenproof dish. Sprinkle the demerara sugar over the top.

5 Place in the heated oven for 15 minutes, until heated through and crisp round the edges. Serve immediately.

When you cannot get dessert gooseberries, use a cooking variety, but you might need to add more sugar. You can make the pancakes a day ahead, let them cool and keep them in the refrigerator in a polythene bag.

Dessert gooseberries with their full flavour and slightly acid tang make a refreshing filling for fans of pancakes with a crisp, sweet demerara topping.